YOUR
FINANCES
IN
CHANGING
TIMES

By Larry Burkett

Illustrations by Dave McGill

Cover Design by Larry Burkett, Jr.

Dedicated To: My wife, Judy

My sons, Larry, Danny and Todd

and

My daughter, Kimberly

Also to my dear Christian friends who helped make this book a reality through their prayers and financial assistance. Charles and Edna Bearden, Greg Brezina, Bill Buck, Sid Cook, Victor Diffee, Bob Field, Hal Hayes, John Haynes, Reid Hughes, Thelma Kerr, Bob Lahr, Dave McGill, Frank McGowan, Vickie Shanahan and all of the other brothers and sisters in Christ whom I forgot to mention but love dearly.

CONTENTS

FOREWORD

This study on Christian finances deals with one of the most important subjects that can occupy the Christian mind today.

Jesus had much to say about money. In fact, more than almost any other subject. It is apparent as I speak to and counsel with many thousands across our country and throughout the world that economics play a major role in the affairs of men and nations. Countries are born and others die because of money or the lack of it. Wars are fought over wealth and ownership of resources.

And yet, few Christians seem to understand the devastation generated through the misuse of money. There are those who have accepted God's financial plan as their own and stand out like giants among their brothers. But, more common is the Christian who withholds this area of his life from God and struggles within the world's financial system. The same frustrations, worries and anxieties which characterize the non-believer are common to many, perhaps most, Christians.

Without a large scale return to God's plan for making, spending and sharing wealth, I fear the same disaster which has overtaken the non-believing world will befall Christians. Outside of God's will we have no immunity to Satan's schemes. Yet we leave ourselves vulnerable to his blows in the realm of finances.

I personally believe that the worldwide economic system is in imminent danger. In the coming changes, *everyone* will be forced to make tremendous financial adjustments. Christians will no longer be able to ride the fence between God and the world. Sunday morning Christianity will no longer be acceptable. While God will provide for those who adhere to His plans, the temptations of the world and the pressures of compromise will lead many Christians to violate God's ordained way to their own detriment and ultimate regret.

Our Lord commands His own to "seek first His (God's) Kingdom and His righteousness," to "lay up . . . treasures in heaven" rather than on earth. This most Christians have failed to do and accordingly have missed the blessing of God while amassing their fortunes.

I believe God's patience is running out, just as it did in the days of Noah. No longer will He allow us to choose a middle-of-the-road existence. Those Christians who seek God will adopt His principles of finance. Those who fail to do so will suffer His chastisement as never before. God will withdraw resources from the poor stewards, as related in Matthew 25, and give it to the good stewards.

No one is immune to financial temptations and difficulties. That is why I endorse this study for every committed Christian seeking God's wisdom. These principles have been verified as only God's Spirit can do: through the changed lives of Christians who have applied them. Countless hundreds of dedicated, sincere Christians who have found themselves victims of Satan's trap have achieved financial freedom through the application of God's plan outlined in this book.

It is God's financial plan that is presented in this study, and I find great diligence has been applied in referencing God's Word to every concept discussed. For this reason this book is a must reading for every Christian who seeks a life of maximum fulfillment for our Lord.

Bill Bright
President and founder
Campus Crusade for Christ

iv

INTRODUCTION

The purpose of this study is to help clarify God's perspective on finances. Too long we have allowed others to influence what we think, feel and believe in this area. It seems that we have lost the point of reference in understanding why we have money and what we are to do with it. Throughout this book, we will focus on what *God* says about handling money.

In the past, this area of study has been largely ignored by both Christian organizations and individuals. Many false conceptions have been introduced about money and Christianity. People hear, "Money is the root of all evil," and believe it comes from Scripture. Indeed it does not. Many people believe that it is inherently spiritual to live in poverty or that there is something innately sinful about having money. Neither is true. These attitudes come from men not God.

Christians have become victims of one of the most devious plots that Satan ever created — the concept that money belongs to us and not to God. Indeed, everything that we own belongs to God — money included — and He will use it to direct our lives.

As we go through this study, we will utilize hundreds of Scriptures dealing with money. It is easy to determine the importance that money plays in God's plan by the abundance of verses that relate to it — there are over 700 direct references to its use.

Many of these references are commonly misinterpreted by people who assume some spiritual principle not directly related to money. That's not totally in error, because often God's Word does contain more than a single lesson. But you should always address the *simplest* meaning *first*. When God speaks about *money*, He means *money*. When He speaks about multiplying assets, that means multiplying financial assets. When He talks about the evils of co-signing, that really means co-signing.

The Search for Answers

In Christian circles, almost everything that is heard relating to money deals with giving and sharing and why God says to do so. Obviously, a part of God's plan for our lives is sharing. But this is not the place God starts; He wants our spiritual commitment first. Once that commitment is made God wants to direct how we make, spend, save, invest and share the money He supplies.

These are the principles we are going to study. We will talk in specifics rather than generalities. Too often when you finish a book on Christian finances, you are left with more doubts and questions than answers. We are going to deal with questions such as:

How should your money be earned?

How does your money affect attitudes?

How does money affect your family?

Is it proper to save money or should you give it away?

Is it proper for a Christian to have insurance?

Is it better to own a home or rent?

Can a Christian be wealthy or is it better to be poor?

We will deal with each of these questions from *God's* perspective.

Application

The emphasis throughout this study is on *application* rather than information. This material will, I believe, become a reference for you to share with hundreds of other Christians what God has to say about money and its uses.

God discusses these areas in Scripture; they are not unspiritual. They are a part of God's plan for our lives.

I sincerely believe that once Christians have been educated in God's plan for their finances, a revolution will occur. Christians will find a freedom they have never known before.

For those who are engaged in making money — as virtually all are — over 80% of the waking day is spent thinking about how to make, save and spend it. Money is such an important subject that nearly two-thirds of the parables that Christ left us deal with the use and handling of it. That alone should tell us the importance of understanding God's plan for finances.

Content

In the course of this study, we will cover many controversial areas; some you will agree with, others you may not. But God's principles of finance are no longer on trial; they have held true over the years. They are not dependent on the economy, or how much money we do or do not have. God's principles depend simply on obedience to His will and turning these areas over to Him.

We will discuss some modern financial devices such as insurance, leverage and investments, as well as different types of credit and how they are used. Some areas will require an interpretation, but that interpretation will be based on a scriptural point of reference wherever used. You are encouraged to study these Scriptures and verify for yourself the principles to which they are applied.

This book is meant to be a complete reference guide on Christian finances, containing important concepts upon which to build a financial program. The principles that are shared should become as familiar to you as your own telephone number. Every time you are faced with a financial decision, they should pop into your mind and should raise mental flags that will tell you whether or not you are handling money God's way.

The Economy

Throughout our society, and particularly in secular business circles, discussions center around the economy and the prospect of future collapse. Most economists believe that although there will be some temporary ups and downs, on the whole, our economy is suffering a malady that has no cure. We are going to discuss that malady, how you can understand it, and how you can be a part of the solution rather than a part of the problem.

Many signs predict an economic disaster—the severity of which has been assessed from a depression, which is a prolonged economic slowdown, to a collapse, which is an absolute halt in our economy. It is difficult to tell how much of either view is true, but as we review our economy, each area will be explored.

One fact is clear: we are facing dire financial and social

crises. Data from every segment of our society bear this out, and it is very clear that Christians living outside God's plan are going to suffer needlessly.

Time Is Short

Part I of this book was included only after much prayer and consultation with other Christians. It is presented to make Christians aware that time to plan and prepare in this economy is short. Whether Christ's return is imminent or not, Christians need to understand exactly what God's financial plan is and the consequences of not following it.

Throughout this study, the reference version of Scripture primarily used is the New American Standard because it is a modern language translation suitable for most Christians.

PART I

THE ECONOMY

CHAPTER ONE

HOW ECONOMIES BEGIN

Times are changing rapidly. Long established economic principles are dissolving, and new economic theories are being born every day. The old "classical" economists are shaking their heads as they discover that they no longer know what is going on and as they realize that the "traditional" techniques of restoring the economy no longer work. The ideas behind cost-push and price demand no longer hold true because we see that prices can rise while production falls off. Employment declines in one segment of the economy while wages rise in another. Why is this? What's happening? What can we expect to happen in the future? These are the questions to be answered in Part I.

Attitudes and Actions

Too often we react to the events around us without understanding what is *really* happening and why. Overreaction is the norm in America today, and in nearly any crisis, the sequence of events is predictable — first, alarm, followed by temporary panic, which, in turn, is followed by apathy and disinterest.

Thus as we look at the future, we tend to overreact and to view it with anxiety and worry. God says that worry is a

1

sin and should not characterize our attitudes. What is worry really? Taking on a responsibility that belongs to someone else.

Unlike the majority of the population (those who are not attuned to God's financial plan), we don't have to be worried by circumstances. God has revealed to us in His Word what has happened and will happen. Parts of the Bible are history, parts are current events, and portions of it are prophecy for tomorrow. Through His Word God tells us what to expect in this economy and how to respond.

I did say *respond* as opposed to *react*. When we respond to something, we bring in the information, check it against known values, and then act accordingly. When we react to something, we bring it in, amplify whatever we receive, and put it back out. That is *not* what God has in mind for us.

As we look at the economy today and where it may be headed tomorrow, we need to view it from the perspective God gives us in His Word. The most important part of that perspective is the imminent return of Christ. When we hear that Christ may return during our time, we say that we believe it. But when God's plan is beginning to be unveiled to us, many refuse to accept it. Seemingly, we react as did the early Christians in Acts 12.

Peter had just been imprisoned and was to be executed. The Christians who traveled with him had retreated to his house to pray. They stayed that entire evening, praying that God would have Peter released from prison unharmed.

Then God performed a miracle and Peter walked out of prison a free man. He went to where the small group was praying and knocked on the gate.

A young girl answered the knock and swung open the gate. There stood Peter. Shocked at the sight of him, she rushed back to the group saying, "Come quickly, Peter stands at the gate!" And what did they do? They chided her. "No, Peter can't be here," they said. "We're praying for him in prison."

Nevertheless, there he stood. They had prayed for a miracle. God had granted their prayer, and yet, they didn't have enough faith to believe it.

Sometimes we are the same way. We *say* that we believe the second coming is near, but when we see the imminent signs, including the changing pulse of the economy, we refuse to accept it.

The Economy

Isolating the economy from any other event, a prudent observer would say that we have a *problem*. Notice that the United States' economy and most of the world's economy is very unstable.

The value of the U. S. dollar is shrinking on the world market. Consequently, most other countries that have depended on our stability in the past are pushed to virtual bankruptcy. The economic balance has shifted to the mideast cartel where little money is actually necessary. What does all this mean and where are we headed?

Obviously, inflation is growing. In recent years it has increased at an alarming rate, while real production has dropped off. Major industries are pursuing a self-preservation attitude — some of them to the brink of disaster. Prices continue to soar while real production declines. Thus a new term has been coined, "inflationary recession" (prices increase while output declines).

HOW ECONOMIES BEGIN

Inflationary recession is not unique in the world economy, but it is unique in the United States. For so long we touted our fiscal controls in the belief that these things couldn't happen here.

It was believed inflation could be halted simply by reducing the money supply and recession could be controlled by the opposite technique. This attitude is no longer credible. If we enter an inflationary period and begin to control the money supply, the economy immediately slips into a recession.  Then, in order to get out, it is necessary to flood the market with additional money which in turn fans the fires of inflation even further.

Economic Trend

These events should alarm those who are at the controls of this sinking ship, because they verify that the highly publicized' controls no longer work. The trend toward economic collapse — where inflation runs away and is followed by major depression — seems irreversible.

Partly responsible for the trend is the lack of fiscal discipline and sound management. These inadequacies reflect an economic system created by popularity. Politicians who make decisions based on what is popular rather than what is financially sound, have virtually bankrupted us.

It is hard to visualize the kind of political climate necessary to reverse this trend.

Rather than working on a feasible solution to our problems, government officials quibble about which group should get the most handouts. They grant price supports to one group, unemployment benefits to another, and gratuities to many people who are really undeserving. They provide grants to New England ski resorts because of insufficient snow one year, then support beaches in the South because of too much rain. They pay people not to grow products in a time of shortage, apply price supports to foods when they begin to drop and then complain of runaway inflation on these same products. The Federal reserve system cuts off credit to industries that are profitable, protesting that they should be more self-sufficient without credit, when for 40 years the system promoted the use of nothing but credit. Nor is the "average" American guiltless either. Most families today live on the brink of disaster. The excessive use of personal and business credit has weakened the already shaky family structure. All of these factors contribute to an almost uncontrollable economy.

Understanding the Economy of Today

In order to understand *where* our economy is, it is first necessary to understand *what* an economy is. Let's back up to an earlier time and see how an economy comes into existence.

If we look back in time, we find that people were basically barterers. Unless every product needed could be grown on one farm, it was necessary for neighbors to swap products.

Let's say, for example, that three individuals live in a certain little community. One raises cows; he's a dairyman. The second is a farmer who raises corn, wheat and barley. The third is a blacksmith who manufactures horseshoes and nails.

HOW ECONOMIES BEGIN

The dairyman decides that he would like to build a barn for his cows. He has lots of timber on his property and so that isn't any problem. He is able to cut down his trees and store his timber until it's cured and ready to use, but he's tired of using wooden pegs to put up his buildings — it's so much trouble to drill holes, pound pegs and sand them down. Then he hit on a plan.

The dairyman used nails to build his barn and was so pleased he decided to get some more to repair his house:

6

He went back to the blacksmith to swap for some more nails:

Perplexed by the blacksmith's refusal, the dairyman turned to his neighbor the farmer for help:

HOW ECONOMIES BEGIN

Swapping his cow for some corn, the dairyman returned to see the blacksmith:

The dairyman repaired his house and began to talk up the virtues of using nails.

Soon other people began coming to the blacksmith to swap their products for nails:

Then the blacksmith had an idea! Why make horseshoes and other stuff? There seemed to be a good business going in nails. So he began to specialize in manufacturing nothing but nails!

As more and more people used nails, Dan developed a flourishing business. Everybody wanted nails to trade. Nails became what we call "money." Money, in any system, must satisfy three basic functions: It must have *value*, it must be *storable*, and it must be *divisible*. Dan's nails satisfied everyone of these aspects and so they were used as money.

Dan had been in business several months when a farmer came by one afternoon with a large order:

When Dan wrote out a paper declaring that he had 100 bags of nails on hand for the farmer, he created a new medium of exchange — *paper money*. This paper money had to satisfy the same basic functions that our original money did to be called *money*, and it did. Nothing new was created by this paper money. It merely represented the nails in storage.

The distribution of paper money rather than nails continued as more and more people discovered that it was eaiser to carry pieces of paper than nails.

Dan began to notice that most of the nails remained in his warehouse. Although they belonged to somebody else, he always had surplus nails.

10

He began to think, "Why should I let these nails sit idle? No sense in making more nails when all these are here."

Then one day a farmer needed some nails but couldn't pay for them right then. So Dan loaned him some nails to be repaid later:

Only this time, rather than making any new nails, he simply issued paper on nails already stored in his warehouse. What had Dan become? A banker! He stored money (nails) for some and loaned it to others.

Dan had also created a new kind of money — *CREDIT!*

Now credit seemed like a good thing. Without even knowing it, others were able to use this credit to build houses and barns. Dan's business prospered through his use of *credit* — other people's money.

HOW ECONOMIES BEGIN

Unfortunately, to keep his business growing, Dan was forced to expand using more and more credit. Then one day a depositor came to collect a large order of nails that Dan was supposed to be storing for him:

Quickly the farmers called a local meeting to compare nail receipts. One had 1,000 bags coming, another 500, etc.

It was obvious that something was wrong!

So they all rushed to Dan's bank and demanded their nails back.

What happened? Dan went bankrupt. Why? Where did he go wrong?

CREDIT was his downfall. When his depositors lost confidence in him, Dan was finished as a banker. He just loaned out too many nails that belonged to *others*. You see, although credit looks like money, it isn't. Credit is storable and divisible but it lacks one essential element — *value*. Credit cost nothing to create.

As we will see later, this same difficulty has occurred in real economics as well. Governments, playing the role of world bankers, have issued credit until few people really believe they can ever repay their debts.

CHAPTER TWO

THE UNITED STATES' ECONOMY

We will begin our discussion of the U. S. economy in the period prior to World War I. In the pre-World War I American economy, the money used was equal to the value of the products being purchased. The dollar (our paper money) was backed by gold or silver (our equivalent of Dan's nails) and was accepted throughout the world without reservation because of great supplies of both. There is nothing inherently of value in gold and silver except that they are relatively scarce and have been accepted as standards of exchange for many thousands of years. A broad generalization of the pre-World War I American economy would be stability.

For every increase in the money supply, something of value was created to back it up. Thus, as the money supply increased, there was an offsetting increase in the product supply.

As the nation approached the 1920's, few businesses relied on credit, but individuals began to use credit to speculate in the stock market. The industrial boom was underway and companies were growing like wildfire. It was thought prosperity was assured. Money had value and the companies were able to expand without real concern for future inflation. But disaster loomed when, through speculation, confidence in the stock market faded.

THE UNITED STATES' ECONOMY

Depression — Speculation

Speculation sparked the Great Depression, not expansion. Expansion was proper as long as it was based on sound value; it was when individuals began to borrow money to speculate in stocks and businesses used this borrowed money to expand, that disaster occurred. When caught in the squeeze, neither was able to pay their bills.

By the late 1920's, the stock market had inflated completely out of proportion. It was being used as a vehicle for "get rich quick" speculation, rather than long term growth.

During the pre-depression era, the banking industry, in spite of the Federal Reserve System controls, was generally unregulated. Just as in Dan's nail bank, few, if any, real controls were enforced. Banks made speculative loans backed by little or no security. They used *credit* to expand, just as Dan, the blacksmith, had.

Then, in 1929, the collapse came. First, it was the stock market which collapsed, followed by large scale loan defaults and almost total economic devastation. Shortly thereafter, banks that were thought stable and had been so for decades, collapsed. Unable to recover their deposits, individuals lost their life savings, and companies lost most of their operating capital. Businesses that were heavily credit-oriented were forced out of existence.

The New Deal

Each new wave of panic created more and more unemployment worldwide as the situation worsened. Then, in the 1930's, the New Deal came into existence, bringing with it stiff government controls and more people on welfare or on the government's payroll.

The government first attempted to fund the increase in money by confiscating private stocks of gold and reissuing paper money. When that was exhausted, the treasury began printing credit-money for the first time. (Affectionately known in monetary circles as "funny money.") This new credit expanded the money supply, but without putting back into the economy something with sound value. It was during this period that the national debt was established.

During the 1940's and World War II, the great national debt was firmly entrenched. Additional capital was created to fund the war effort, while products were consumed by the millions and billions of tons.

CONSUMER CREDIT

In the 1950's the onslaught of consumer credit, and the reconstruction of Europe by the United States began. Hundreds of billions of dollars were spent in rebuilding the war-torn countries in Europe and Asia.

The consumer credit boom generated trillions of dollars in new money. The post World War II housing boom in the United States provided millions of houses on credit, and through the use of credit, banking channels again expanded drastically. More supports were instituted by the government with more taxes being extracted to pay for welfare, Social Security and government employment.

Paper Prosperity

The 1960's were thought to be years of endless prosperity. Few people thought that the boom would actually disappear. Europe began to adopt the credit system the United States had triggered, and individual credit cards, personal credit and business debt grew astronomically. As the money supply grew faster and faster, the product supply struggled to keep up. Production showed signs of difficulties and began to level off rather than climb, while the debt continued to accelerate.

Then, in the 1970's reality appeared. Worldwide, we began to suffer pollution because of the rapid industrialization that came about in the 1940's, 50's, and 60's. For the first time, shortages in basic commodities were apparent. Inflation, sparked by this rapid expansion of the money supply, became a critical statistic. More and more subsidies became necessary, with almost every major industry in the United States receiving government aid. Consequently more new money was created to fund the subsidies. Foreign governments began to lack confidence in American currency and seek other security in international trade.

THE UNITED STATES' ECONOMY

Current Situation

The dollar is no longer the standard for exchange throughout the world, and larger amounts of American currency are necessary due to this lack of confidence. Where will it all end? It is difficult to assess the exact changes, but with some reasoning, I believe it is possible to determine the *direction* we are going.

The Inflation Spiral

Technological changes in the United States occur on a scale that boggles the mind; new products are introduced every day. But even though production is high in the United States, so is inflation. As the situation worsens, new theories develop and the government generates ideas to control recession—and then has to fight inflation. Unfortunately, all of these ideas are treating *symptoms,* and none are treating *problems.*

If the economy is in an inflationary spiral, the controls choke off the money supply (primarily credit) in an attempt to stop the increases. The effect of this is to stifle those segments of the economy that are dependent on credit, as most are. The economy then plunges into a recessionary period, and it takes greater quantities of money to reverse that trend. Each time the economy inflates, it generates higher prices. Each time it deflates, it picks up higher unemployment. What does the future hold for us economically? We will explore this in the next chapter.

CHAPTER THREE

THE CASHLESS SYSTEM

The important questions are: What can we expect in the future and what kind of decisions can we make based on those expectations? To answer these questions, it is necessary to make some assumptions and observations.

Future Economic Trends

I believe we are going to see ever intensifying recessionary and inflationary spirals. During the inflationary periods, Americans will experience higher and higher prices. These prices will be caused by more and more money being created and disbursed into the market, with fewer and fewer products being produced to offset this new money. Government controls will expand, causing increased subsidies with fewer people contributing. Combined with the higher prices will be higher taxes.

During the recessions, more individuals will become unemployed as basic industries contract. Many of these people will be added to the government payrolls in an effort to appease those being hurt by the system. I believe we will develop what might be termed "shear economy." In a shear economy, one segment will boom while another will be in a bust. Workers in the boom industries will be

able to demand higher wages, while those in a bust industry will be laid off. The unemployed will then demand
compensation from the government,
which will step in with subsidies,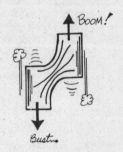
welfare and job supports, thus creat-
ing the need for more money to be
put back into the system.

It is easy to envision shortages in
industries involving fuel, food and
shelter. As other nations of the world,
such as the oil countries, demand
higher levels of affluence for their
people, we must begin to relinquish some of our affluence
to compensate.

In this situation, more people will depend on the government for the answers (perhaps even a national hysteria
in which the government is expected to make virtually
every decision).

Pressure groups will chastise government leaders whenever they make wrong decisions. Consequently officials will
become less prone to make *any* decisions, but when forced
to act, they will be more prone to just treat the symptom
and pacify the people, whatever the cost. During the recessions, they will spend all the money necessary to
reverse the cycle. In inflationary spirals, leaders will try to
appease the people by giving them something "for
nothing." The attitude will be to deal with whatever
happens to exist at that time. It will become almost a
necessity for the government to have total control of
the money supply through some form of nationalization
of the banking interests.

Will we ever have another great depression or a collapse?
I don't know but I do know that we are evolving into a
new system, perhaps precipitated by a collapse. No matter
what happens, we will have another "new deal" — one
that people will ask for because of devastating problems
(high prices, high unemployment, money almost worthless

because of inflation and the prospect of a crime epidemic).

The New System

I believe that ultimately we can look for a new, *cashless* system. If indeed the present system collapsed and we had high prices even in the midst of that collapse, people would begin to get hysterical and even riot, stealing what they wanted. The government would be forced to step in and establish some kind of control, which could best be set up by stopping the flow of money temporarily and then reorganizing the monetary system totally. It would have to be virtually dictatorial under government control so that the new economic system could operate on a cashless or credit card system.

I believe that initially each individual will be issued a number of digits (or units) for the amount of money held in the bank and proportional to earnings. A master credit card will be used to make most or all purchases. Eventually, as the system progresses, there will be no money, only a credit card per individual. The card will be checked through the electronic cash register at the store and also against a central computer to determine allocation of credit so that no one will be able to borrow beyond his ability to repay, nor will anyone be able to accumulate excessive amounts of money. It is conceivable that each individual will have a definite accumulation limit so that no large surpluses will exist. Profits may be allowed in business, but they will be contained within the maximums that the government prescribes.

Additionally, crime could be drastically reduced through this system, since crime prevention will become one of the major goals of the government. As the economy continues to slip, the cashless system will be an important tool in the battle against criminals. Money thefts will become a thing of the past because there will be *no* money.

THE CASHLESS SYSTEM

It will be fruitless to rob banks because all they will store are computer tapes. It will make no sense to kidnap someone either, because the criminal could only have his account credited. Retail store thefts will be reduced to product losses only. Thus, two major problems could be solved at one time — crime reduced and a common medium of exchange established throughout the world. I believe that whatever system is enacted, it will of necessity be worldwide, thereby creating a common medium of exchange.

The Flaw in the System

The only factor left to deal with is the credit card itself. Because credit cards could be destroyed, lost, counterfeited or forged, the credit card black market would soon become a major problem. A functional and workable system to do away with the credit card would be to indelibly imprint on each individual a number equivalent to his credit card number that could not be forged or altered. Perhaps a magnetic ink number tattooed just under the skin. The number could be detected by an electronic scanner and verified against the central computer at any time.

THE CASHLESS SYSTEM

Is a Cashless System Possible?

This cashless system may seem farfetched to those unacquainted with monetary trends, but even a cursory investigation clearly establishes the fact that systems similar to the one presented here are now being tested throughout the United States and Europe in contemplation of a totally "cashless" system of banking. Virtually no one in major banking circles will deny either the necessity of such a system or its future certainty. In fact, the world bank has already begun work on a massive computer system that will be used to catalog and categorize every individual in the world.

What does all this mean to us and how does this relate to Christian finances? This is the kind of system that *must* exist prior to the Age of Apostasy in the last days. It must be a system so subtle that people will ask for it and, unless they are aware, even the "elect" may be deceived. Let's now go to God's Word and begin to look at what He says about this age, how it affects Christians, and what He expects us to do.

CHAPTER FOUR

GOD'S TIMETABLE

In these rapidly changing times, it is important for Christians to understand what is happening, why it is happening, and what can be expected according to God's Word. We have reviewed the economy from a secular viewpoint in order to understand *how* a basic economy works.

Now we will look to God's Word for answers to our questions about the future. It is *vital* for Christians to understand what God says and why. I believe God has revealed to us every aspect of the economy for the time in which we are living.

Time is a scroll to God. Through His Word, He unrolls the scroll and reveals the past, present and future to us. So it is important when studying God's Word to remember that He is infinite and timeless, and although it may seem to us that He tarries, His plan *will be completed.*

A Prophet's View

To begin our look into God's Word, let's review some of the visions of the prophets. It is important to remember that these men in many cases were writing about things they really did not understand. For instance, when God

24

revealed the events in the last days to Daniel, he had difficulty describing them. We now know that when Christ comes again, it will be in at least the 20th century, therefore, the things that God revealed to Daniel he could not possibly understand. Perhaps it was a revelation of rockets, airplanes, televisions and automobiles. Can you imagine your own difficulty under the same circumstances?

When Jeremiah wrote of seeing the arrows of the enemy strike to the heart of Babylon, these arrows could well have been missiles. When Daniel described "many will go back and forth," think of it as Daniel must have: seeing jet aircraft and powered machines running to and fro across the world.

Daniel also wrote, "And knowledge will increase." Envision how it must have seemed to him as he looked into the future, for knowledge has increased immeasurably in the 20th century. And remember, too, that as the prophets wrote these visions from God, they had to describe them in the vernacular of their day. So as you read these events think of them in relation to the time in which we live.

God wants Christians to check everything against His Word. If it parallels what He says in His Word, we should have no anxiety, worry or fear. Remember, God *is* in control. He is the creator and master of the universe. It is *His* plan that is being unfolded right before our eyes. What an exciting time we live in! We are the only generation, other than perhaps that of the first century Christians, which has any real reason to believe that Christ's return is near.

The Falling Away

There are many events that tell us the Age of Apostasy is approaching. This section will deal with the events of that age as I see them and how I believe they relate to our economy. I am not a prophet in any sense of the Word except that God, through His Holy Spirit, promises to reveal the truth to us. He then commands that we must reveal the truth to others. He says to let those who have insight advise others, and *everyone* can have insight. God promises it to all who seek His kingdom and His mind.

As stated before, even in view of signs that point to the imminent return of Christ, many refuse to act as He directs. God does have things that He expects from each of us, but too often we see events that are happening from our own perspective, rather than from His. It is important to understand God's revelation and begin to share it with others. Future events will demand drastic adjustments in our finances and strict adherence to God's plan. Events that cause alarm for non-Christians (the disintegration of the economy, the chaos that exists in the world today, the lawlessness and the astounding rise in immorality) should bring the Christians into closer fellowship. Although Christians should not rejoice in these things, we should rejoice in the fact that God declared through His Word these things would happen. When these events occur, He says, be alert and be aware lest you be deceived, for Christ *is* coming again.

Difficult times throughout history have brought Christians closer together. And whether Christ comes this year, next year or a thousand years from now, we *are* facing difficult times. This period should make committed

Christians aware of how temporal things of the world are and how helpless each and every one of us is outside of God's will and direction.

God expects *action* from us. Yet, He never asks us to do anything without both the time and the means to do so. We can claim that promise even in these difficult times.

God's plan is that His Word be spread unto all the world. A part of that plan requires Christians to have enough resources for their needs and an abundance to spread the gospel. Therefore, we can be sure that if we manage His money properly, He will multiply it and give us enough so that we can share freely. "Give, and it will be given to you; good measure, pressed down, shaken together, running over, they will pour into your lap. For whatever measure you deal out to others, it will be dealt to you in return" (Luke 6:38, New American Standard).

Are These "The Last Days"?

At this point, I'd like to share some of the things that speak loudly to me from Scripture and, I believe, clearly reveal the last days.

First, many lessons for the United States today can be found in the directions God gave the nation of Israel.

Second, we can identify many signs that speak of Christ's return. He said, "This generation will not pass away until all these things take place" (Matthew 24:34).

Third, God says we should be aware for there will be a great deal of deception (Matthew 24). As I studied these signs, several factors became apparent:

1. Great deception will abound in the last days.
2. People will be confused about whether the last days are upon them.
3. They will argue about whether the signs are true.

27

GOD'S TIMETABLE

Through the ages, people have scoffed at God's Word, and many have said, "These signs have been in existence before." Although, we know that *some* signs have been in existence since Christ's departure, we also know from God's Word that in the last days, *all* of these signs will converge together. I personally believe that *most* of the signs are in existence today, far more than have ever existed before. Too often we find Christians engaged in discussions as to whether or not they will face tribulations in the end times. It would be far better for Christians to prepare for tribulation and never have to face it, than to be unprepared in the midst of it.

I believe from God's Word that the last generation of Christians will face great difficulties. These difficulties could be catastrophic if met unprepared. God says that many will fall away, turning from Him because they will be caught unaware. I always think back to the third century Christians. Many of them were dipped in oil, tied to posts and set on fire to light the gardens of Rome. It was said that the hills of Rome glowed with their burning bodies. To a Christian just dipped in oil and set on fire, it was academic whether that was a great or a minor tribulation!

Scriptural Parallels

As previously mentioned, I believe many parallel lessons can be drawn between America's growth and the nation of Israel. The United States is the most materially blessed nation that has ever existed. We have more wealth per individual and more trained Christians than any other nation on the earth has ever had.

In Deuteronomy 8:11, God gave a warning saying, "Beware lest you forget the Lord your God by not keeping His commandments and His ordinances and His statutes which I am commanding you today. " A review of Jewish history shows that happened scores of times.

I see a parallel in the history of the United States. America began on the precepts of a godly nation. Most of our forefathers were committed to the teachings of the Scripture. Three times the Constitution states that they yielded their power to God Almighty. But, sadly, in our country we have drifted away from this philosophy. We are now basically an atheistic system, even hampering prayer in public schools.

Further in Deuteronomy 28:12, 13, God says, "The Lord will open for you His good storehouse, the heavens, to give rain to your land in its seasons and to bless all of the work of your hand; and you shall lend to many nations, but you shall not borrow. And the Lord will make you the head and not the tail, and you only shall be above, and you shall not be underneath, if you will listen to the commandments of the Lord your God, which I charge you today, to observe them carefully." Look back at the history of America. Did we not lend to every nation on the face of this earth and borrow from none? For nearly 200 years, we have been the most affluent nation on earth.

What has happened? Have we slipped from God's path? I believe we have the answer in Deuteronomy 28:15 and 28:43. "But it shall come about, if you will not obey the Lord your God . . .," and "The alien who is among you shall rise above you higher and higher, but you shall go down lower and lower."

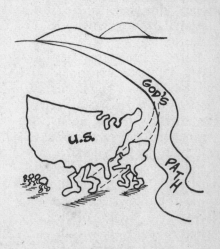

In the Living Bible it says, "Foreigners living among you shall become richer and richer while you become poorer and poorer. They shall lend to you, not you to them! They shall be the head and you shall be the tail!"

It is obvious that this *is* happening, for massive amounts of currency are coming into the United States from foreign countries. I recall a headline in one of the national newspapers that read, "Arab Money, Not Oil, Pours into the United States." The story told about the foreign currency pouring into the United States. It said that 10 nation members of the organization of petroleum exporting companies had collected approximately $60 billion more than they needed. The World Bank calculated that the surplus could grow to more than a trillion dollars by the end of 1980 — that is 10 times more than the United States has invested abroad.

Much of this money from other countries is being poured back into the United States. Foreigners are lending to America's businesses at an unparalleled rate. Industries caught in economic downturns are looking for sources of money anywhere. So foreign governments are pouring money into land, banking interests, corporations, airlines and military productivity in this country.

Most of the financiers and real estate experts in the world have predicted that a large portion of the surplus of oil money throughout the world will end up in the United States, Europe, Canada, Japan and Australia. They predict the United States will reap large harvests in terms of invested capital from outside, but I question from God's

Word whether events such as these are harvests or reapings of what has been sown. For we see the foreigner living among us becoming richer while we get poorer and poorer. Talk to people around you, to bankers and investors, about the flow of foreign currency into the United States. The figures are astronomical.

Physical Signs

There are many great Christians alive today who believe that this is indeed the generation in which Christ will return. I personally believe these are the last days and am convicted to plan accordingly. However, each Christian must decide personally whether to believe or not. No one can predict when Christ is coming again. In Matthew 24:36, our Lord says, "But of that day and hour no one knows, not even the angels of heaven, nor the Son, but the Father alone." But then He states, "Learn the parable from the fig tree: when its branch has already become tender, and puts forth its leaves, you know that summer is near; even so you too, when you see all these things, recognize that He is near, right at the door" (Matthew 24:32, 33). "These things are merely the beginning of birthpangs" (Matthew 24:8). We need to be aware to be able to decide for ourselves whether these are the last days.

We need to know the physical signs for the last days and how these signs will appear. This is not intended to be an all-inclusive study of the last days, but a study of the signs I believe to be most apparent. I think these signs also help us to envision what changes are necessary in our economy for it to become one for the last days.

A. *The first sign* is the destruction of Jerusalem prophesied in Ezekiel. That was accomplished in 70 A. D.

B. *The second* is found in Matthew 24:7: "For nation will rise against nation, and kingdom against kingdom." I believe that this prophecy was fulfilled by the First World

War. It was started by two minor nations, Austria and Serbia, and expanded into a conflict involving virtually every nation on earth.

C. *The third physical sign* is the reconstruction of the nation of Israel, which was actually begun in 1916 (at the conclusion of World War I) and accomplished in 1948 (Ezekiel 37).

D. *The fourth sign* is found in Daniel's description of people running to and fro across the world (Daniel 12). This was accomplished during the mid-20th century and goes on even today.

E. *The fifth sign* predicts that knowledge shall increase (Daniel 12). Prior to the 20th century, man lived basically the same as in the previous 5,000 years. But from the turn of the 20th century until today, man's knowledge has increased a hundredfold.

Medical knowledge has increased to the point that removal and replacement of vital organs is almost routine. In electronics, our knowledge has increased to the point that computers think in terms of billionths of a second with storage capacities that rival the human brain.

Transportation has advanced to the stage that a trip from the East to the West Coast (requiring at least three months 75 years ago) now takes less than four hours. It is not unknown today for someone to live in one country and work in another. Indeed, man is able to run to and fro as never before. And knowledge has increased to a point that men challenge God's authority over nature. It is incredible to observe these things evolving from the written Word of God and still ignore the fact that His hand is upon us and that Christ is indeed coming again. By no means are these all the physical signs leading to Christ's return, but they are so predominant as to be astounding.

Prophetic Signs

Perhaps the clearest pictures of the last days are presented in Matthew 24 and Luke 21. Combine these with the apostolic views given in I and II Thessalonians and they provide insight into the period called the Age of Apostasy. I have briefly summarized some points which outline these prophecies.

Sign	Scriptures
1. Fear will overtake most of the world.	Matthew 24:6 and Luke 21:9
2. Many will be misled during these days.	Matthew 24:5; Matthew 24:24 and Luke 21:8
3. There will be wars and rumors of war.	Matthew 24:6 and Luke 21:9
4. There will be famines, earthquakes and plagues.	Matthew 24:7 and Luke 21:11
5. There will be many betrayals.	Matthew 24:10
6. There will be great lawlessness during this time.	Matthew 24:12 and II Thessalonians 2:7
7. Men will hold to a form of godliness but not the true God.	II Timothy 3:5
8. There will be great immorality during those days.	I Timothy 4:3 and II Timothy 3:2
9. When the fig tree blooms, understand that these things are at hand.	Matthew 24:32 and Luke 21:29
10. There will be great love of money in those days.	II Timothy 3:2

GOD'S TIMETABLE

11.	There will be great deception	II Thessalonians 2:9 and I Timothy 4:1
12.	There will be need for an awareness of Christ's return	Matthew 24:33; Matthew 24:42, 43; Luke 21:36 and I Thessalonians 5:6
13.	It will be business as usual.	Matthew 24: 37-39 and I Thessalonians 5:3
14.	Those who are in the cities must flee to the mountains.	Matthew 24:16-20 and Luke 21:21.
15.	The mark of the Beast will be used.	Revelation 13:16, 17 and 14:9-11

These prophetic signs, combined with the previously mentioned physical signs, point the way to Christ's return—if we can decipher what they mean.

1. *Fear.*

God admonishes us not to be afraid. This admonition is necessary even for Christians. Because God realizes that when we become aware of these signs our reaction will be fear and anxiety.

2. *Deceivers.*

God warns that many will be misled and will fall away, "For many will come in My name, saying, 'I am the Christ,' and will mislead many" (Matthew 24:5). Today's generation has scores and scores of deceiving heretics who come saying that Christ's death was an error, others claiming to be Christ Himself, and still others teaching another salvation. These false prophets deceive millions who lack spiritual discernment.

3. *Wars.*

God states there will be wars and rumors of wars. This is true throughout the whole world, but particularly in an area where it would have seemed impossible to have such a situation 50 years ago, the Middle East.

34

4. *Famines—Earthquakes.*

Christ states there will be famines on the face of the earth and many earthquakes. It is predicted that as many as 200 million people will starve to death between 1975 and 1980. There have been earthquakes across the world before, but there have been more in the 20th century than in all of previously recorded history. The Scripture predicts unparalleled catastrophies leading into the last days.

A news article in a Washington paper entitled "Los Angeles Quake Is Predicted" stated that a major earthquake, perhaps the largest in the history of the world, is predicted along the California coast about 1982. I don't presume to be a geologist, but I have read that throughout the whole Pacific Ocean Basin, particularly in California where the fault line runs, great pressures are being built up that can ultimately result in a devastating earthquake of unparalleled magnitude.

5. *Betrayals.*

God says in Matthew 24:10, "And at that time many will fall away and will betray one another . . . . " Many *have* fallen away from the faith. Even in our country, where originally we were committed to the precept that God was imminent, that is no longer true. The gullible are being misled through the promotion of many "cult" religions that don't believe in God.

6. *Lawlessness.*

In Matthew 24:12, Christ states, "And because lawlessness is increased, most people's love will grow cold." Lawlessness has increased throughout the world as well as in the United States. Government statistics report that violent crimes like armed robbery and rape are increasing 17—20% per year and are anticipated to go higher.

7. *A Form of Godliness.*

It is also said that they will hold to a form of godliness (II Timothy 3:5). This is happening in the world today; look at all the "religions" in America. Cults have grown in vast numbers. Many of these promote satanic worship; others promote the worship of sex or violence. Some even profess a belief in God, but it's a human god, one that's understandable and attainable by human efforts.

8. *Immorality.*

A drastic rise in immorality is predicted. Today homosexuals are accepted into society and into the "church" as well; groups that forbid marriage and others that advocate abstaining from certain foods (I Timothy 4:3) also exist. These are the very things that God says will happen in the last days. Pre-marital sex is so widely accepted today that unwed mothers can be found in nearly every high school. Sex education is taught in schools in an effort, it is reported, to keep students from spreading venereal disease, which has reached epidemic proportions in the United States and around the world.

9. *The Fig Tree.*

God also says, "Now learn the parable from the fig tree: when its branch has already become tender, and puts forth its leaves, you know that summer is near" (Matthew 24:32). I believe this parable refers to the nation of Israel, and the fig tree has begun to bloom again. In fact, it is blooming broadly in the Middle East. Look at an aerial photograph of the Middle East, and you will see that Israel is indeed a flower, a great bloom in the midst of that dry, arid land. Remarkable enough, a fig leaf is part of the Israeli flag's emblem.

10. *Great Riches.*

God also says that love of money will abound. "For many will be lovers of self, lovers of money, boastful, arrogant, revilers, disobedient to parents, ungrateful and unholy" (II Timothy 3:2). Does this sound like our society? People today *are* lovers of money and self. We have elevated money to the position of idolatry as never before.

11. *Deceptions.*

Scripture talks of great deceptions during the last days as one of the other signs. "But the Spirit explicitly says that in the later times some will fall away from the faith, paying attention to deceitful spirits and doctrines of demons" (I Timothy 4:1). This generation has become subject to the doctrine of demon worship on a large scale. Demonic worship has been known before in history, but never on the scale we will experience if the present trend continues. There is a rise in the occult movement across the face of the earth, with occults taught in high schools, colleges and universities in America. Classes on demonology and witchcraft are a part of most community colleges' curricula; the interest in astrology is unparalleled even for the times of Babylon.

12. *Be Aware.*

In Matthew 24:42, the Scripture says, "Therefore be on the alert, for you do not know which day your Lord is coming." In these times, Christians must be aware, keeping their eyes on God and not on the world. They must not allow their lives to be manipulated by those around them, but must depend on God's Word for direction.

13. *Business as Usual.*

In Matthew 24:37-39, we read, "For the coming of the Son of Man will be just like the days of Noah. For as in those days which were before the flood they were eating and drinking, they were marrying and giving in marriage, until the day that Noah entered the ark, and they did not understand until the flood came and took them all away, so shall the coming of the Son of Man be." This is an important reference, because, as we review these signs of apostasy, it does not sound like business as usual. Instead, it sounds like chaos throughout the world, and indeed that's what it will be. But the last days *will be* like all other days because people will grow callous and harden their hearts and spirits so much that chaos will be accepted as commonplace. That is why God warns us not to be deceived, but to be aware, because we won't know the day in which Christ comes, for it will seem just like any other day. Most people *will* adjust to the times and accept apostasy as normal.

14. *Flee to the Mountains.*

Scripture says in Matthew 24:16-20, "Then let those who are in Judea flee to the mountains; let him who is on the housetop not go down to get the things that are in his house; and let him who is in the field not turn back to get his cloak. But woe to those who are with child and to those who nurse babes in those days! But pray that your flight may not be in the winter, or on a Sabbath . . . ." God is telling us that some will *have* to flee.

At least those in Judea will flee when the great army marches against the nation of Israel. Who would have believed only three decades ago that the nation of Israel could ever become a viable source of conflict? And yet, today great armies are being amassed that will be used against Israel, perhaps because of the world oil situation. There is also another great hoard of treasure that would make it worth somebody's while to march against Israel — the Dead Sea. It is now estimated that between six and seven trillion dollars worth of minerals can be extracted from this inland ocean. Several Israeli neighbors have been eyeing this treasure with growing resentment.

The Last Sign

We have looked into some of the prophetic areas of Scripture; not into what is *going* to happen, I believe, but into what *is* happening. God says that each of us can understand these things. When they happen, we are to be aware and to tell others. How does the last sign fit into our study? It is the key to tie our study of the economy together. . .

CHAPTER FIVE

SIGN OF THE BEAST — THE NUMBER SYSTEM

What is the sign of the beast, and how does it relate to our earlier discussion on the economy? There should be no doubt in your mind that our economy is changing. Our economic system *must* eventually evolve into a new system because, as long as symptoms are being treated, the *problems* will intensify.

As I said before, I believe the new economic system will be a *cashless* one. Initially, it will be based on credit cards, and then, ultimately, a number (the equivalent of the credit card) to be imprinted on each individual. This, viewed outside of the prophetic Scripture from God, seems harmless. After all, what could be harmful about a credit card? And what could be more logical than to replace a credit card which could be stolen, destroyed or counterfeited, with a number stamped on each individual? It would be permanent, invisible and socially acceptable; it would be practical and progressive.

How does this number relate to what Scripture says will happen? The number represents one more step into the last days. In Revelation 6:6 there is a reference to prices: "And I heard as it were a voice in the center of the four living creatures saying, 'A quart of wheat for a denarius, and three quarts of barley for a denarius; and do not harm the oil and the wine.' " A quart of wheat will cost the equivalent of a whole day's wages. Leading into those days will be high prices, economic problems and shortages.

The 13th chapter of Revelation identifies the sign of the beast. I believe we can draw a straight line from the cashless system and the number that replaces the credit card to the sign of the beast. Revelation 13:16, 17 begins, "And he causes all, the small and the great, and the rich and the poor, and the free men and the slaves, to be given a mark on their right hand, or on their forehead, and he provides that *no one* should be able to buy or to sell, except that one who has the mark, either the name of the beast or the number of his name."

It becomes evident that this prophetic Scripture defines that, without this number, you cannot buy or sell. It is an *economic* number, in addition to any other use. We know from God's own Word that in the last days this system *must* ultimately come to pass. In a free market economy like the United States, or even in an economy that uses money, this could not happen. Because so long as money in any form exists, people can transact freely outside the number system. In order to evolve to this system, the economy must be totally and absolutely *cashless*.

Perilous Times

Revelation 14:9 describes what happens to those who accept the number: "And another angel, a third one, followed them, saying with a loud voice, 'If any one worships the beast and his image, and receives the mark on his forehead or upon his hand, he also will drink of the wine of the wrath of God.' " Thus God gives this admonition: no Christian can be marked with the sign of the beast. I personally believe that the persecution described against

Christians will not originally be religious in nature; it will be economic. Why? Because Christians, as a group, will not go along with the number system.

Economic persecution is not unique, even to this century, particularly in the face of financial crisis. In pre-World War II Germany, Hitler first began to persecute the *entrepreneurs,* those people who controlled the businesses and industries during the German collapse of the 1920's. After discovering that a great percentage of them were Jewish, he transferred that hostility over to anti-Semitism. It is possible that the same will be true for Christians throughout the world. The discovery that the majority of those who will not go along with this number system are Christians could cause a shift of the hostility from economics to religion.

An Alternative to "the System"

What will Christians do during these days? How will we live outside of the system? These questions are important because they set the stage for the rest of our study dealing with Christian finances.

We will live and share as a *body.* In this body will be some with great resource and some with little. The plan that God has chosen is the same one He revealed to the first generation of Christians. Have you ever wondered why God allowed the first century Christians to believe so strongly that Christ would return in their day? Well I have, until God's plan became apparent to me. God allowed the *first* generation to be deceived so that they would develop His plan for the *last* generation.

It is the very plan developed in the Bible that will be used during the last days. Obviously, we cannot wait until the times are upon us to act; it will be too late then. God expects us to act *now* and align our finances according to His plan.

Christians living outside of God's plan will find great difficulty in surviving without the system. But Christians living inside God's plan will have all of their needs met. God promises very clearly that He will not allow us to become impoverished. He will always provide our "sufficiency." To claim this promise, however, we must bring our finances under His authority. We must understand God's plan so thoroughly that it becomes indelibly written in our personalities. Thus, when faced with financial decisions, we no longer react the way the world demands, but respond according to God's plan.

And again, I re-emphasize that whether you believe these are the *last days* or not is not an issue. This economy is changing and changing quickly; it is important that Christians return to the point of reference — God's Word. We must begin to handle our finances according to His timeless plan. When we do so, God *promises* to supply our every need, which He expresses in Psalms 50:14,15: "Offer to God a sacrifice of thanksgiving, and pay your vows to the Most High; and call upon Me in the day of trouble; I shall rescue you, and you will honor Me."

This promise, along with many others we will study, is available to anyone who has accepted Christ as their personal Savior and obeys His commands. If any reader has not made a personal acceptance of the Lord Jesus Christ into his heart, I encourage you to do so right now. It is a simple task that will be a life-changing experience. You will receive the power of God Himself into your life. John 1:12 gives God's promise, "But as many as received Him, to them He gave the right to become children of God, even to those who believe in His name."

You can receive Christ right now simply by asking Him

to come into your life. God knows your heart. He is not concerned with your words; He is concerned with your *attitude*. The following is a suggested prayer that you might use: "Lord Jesus, I need You. I open the door of my life and receive You as my Savior and Lord. Thank You for forgiving my sins. Take control of the throne of my life and make me the kind of person You want me to be."

If you prayed this and you meant it, you can be sure that Christ is in your heart and that God *is* in control of your life. I John 5:11-13 says, "And the witness is this, that God has given us eternal life, and this life is in His Son. He who has the Son has the life; he who does not have the Son of God does not have the life. These things I have written to you who believe in the name of the Son of God, in order that you may know you have eternal life."

PART II

GOD'S PRINCIPLES

OF

FINANCE

CHAPTER SIX

WHAT IS WEALTH?

Since the beginning of man's history he has suffered from His own greed and inability to obey God. Even in the Garden of Eden, Adam and Eve disobeyed God and were cast out to earn their own way. In Genesis 3:19, God says, "By the sweat of your face you shall eat bread." From that day until Christ returns again, man will be concerned with the acquiring and managing of possessions.

It would be accurate to say that most individual tension, family friction, strife, anger and frustration are caused directly or indirectly by money. Over 80% of the waking day for the average individual is spent thinking about, talking about and in pursuit of money.

This area is of great importance to God, too. As we discussed earlier, it is of such importance that the Bible has hundreds of Scripture verses dealing with *how to handle money.*

For the Christian seeking God's best, He has established simple, basic principles in the Bible for the management of possessions. Just as a Christian cannot experience the fullness of the Holy Spirit until he surrenders ownership of his life to Christ, so too, he cannot experience peace in the area of finances until he has surrendered total control of this area to God and accepted his position as a steward.

A steward is one who manages another's resources. Each

WHAT IS WEALTH?

of us is a manager, *not an owner.* God is the owner, and we are to manage according to *His* plan. All of the promises that God has made regarding His blessings in this area are predicated on the principle that we relinquish ownership, and a Christian who refuses to do this can never experience God's plan for his finances. As a consequence, his life will be constantly characterized by turmoil and frustration, anxiety and worry in the area of money.

Wealth—Attitude—God

What is wealth or money? What is the proper attitude toward that wealth? How is God's will expressed in the area of finances?

I recall a story I once read written by the chief accountant for one of the wealthiest men who ever lived—John D. Rockefeller, Sr. In this article, someone asked the accountant, "How much did John D. leave? We know he was an immensely wealthy man." And the accountant answered, "Everything." God would have us remember that we all leave *everything.*

The book of Ecclesiastes deals with stewardship and a principle that Solomon found valid—regardless of his station in life, man accumulates nothing. For each person's wealth and possessions amount to *nothing* upon his death. As we look into the New Testament Scripture, we see that God admonishes us not to "lay up for yourselves treasures upon earth, . . . but lay up for yourselves treasures in heaven" (Matthew 6:19,20).

What Is Wealth?

A review of past civilizations shows that wealth has often been based on the number of cattle or camels owned, land possessed, oil owned and many other material possessions.

WHAT IS WEALTH?

In the early economy of the United States, wealth was related to how much land one owned. Later, wealth related to resources such as gold or silver or other natural elements in the earth. Then it changed again. During the Industrial Revolution it related to how much one had accumulated in worldly goods—namely money.

In our economy today, wealth is still related to money, but the position one holds is also a measure of wealth. Professional men such as doctors, attorneys, dentists and others are thought to be "wealthy" because of their income-earning potential.

A doctor, for example, coming right out of residency is capable of borrowing great amounts of money to go into business without any collateral other than his education. What is his credit based on? His potential productivity. Therefore, even the talents and the abilities that we have are part of our wealth, as is our credit or borrowing ability.

Creation and Uses of Wealth

According to our attitude, wealth can be creative; it can be used to spread God's Word, build hospitals and churches, feed the poor, take care of orphans, etc. Or it can be wasted, spent on frivolous activities, lavish living, gambling, or any other foolish activity. Wealth also can be corruptive, used to purchase influence, bribes, illegal businesses, or guns and bombs.

For the Christian, wealth is that which God entrusts to each of us. From the world's perspective, the creation of wealth evolves around many things, including self-will —how much self-control and will power one has to devote to earning money.

As we will see later, that is not God's perspective because, in every instance, individuals who spend their lives in the pursuit of money end up frustrated and miserable. They never really understand *why* they have money, and as they get closer to death, they realize how futile the attaining of wealth was.

There is a lot of *worldly folklore* surrounding this area called *wealth*. You will recognize some of it here:

1.   *It takes breaks to get ahead.* Whoever gets the best breaks or has the most influence in this world is termed "the guy who gets ahead."

2.   *It takes money to make money.* In other words, the rich get richer.

3.   *You can't be too honest and get ahead today.* Why? You must be willing to shade the truth. If you're extremely honest with people, then you will not be able to deal with the world system.

None of these are God's principles and, in actuality, are nonsense put out by those who seek to rationalize their behavior. The creation of wealth is both a gift and a talent. For some, acquiring wealth is easier than it is for others. But it is possible for anyone who is willing to sacrifice and to achieve by setting and reaching goals.

No, I'm not suggesting that this is good, because as we will see in God's plan, it's *attitude,* not *aptitude* that He honors. The gaining of wealth as an end in itself is a very poor investment of a life. Because, *first,* it requires a great deal of time—to the virtual exclusion of everything else including family, friends, hobbies and relaxation.

Second, there is no correlation between wealth and happiness. That is an important key! There is absolutely *no* correlation between wealth and happiness. Many Christians I observe are inwardly disturbed by the existence of prosperous non-Christians. Yet we

should recognize that Satan is the prince of this world, and it would be an extremely poor recruiting practice if he recruited only the impoverished.

But there is a great difference between God and Satan in our finances. "It is the blessing of the *Lord* that makes rich, and He adds *no sorrow to it* " Proverbs 10:22. This Scripture establishes the foundation for the remainder of our study—*how to have wealth without worry* (wealth being everything that we own: our money, our family, our creative ability—*everything* we have acquired since we arrived and everything we must leave when we go).

Thus we should remember that money is *temporary*. The importance of money to God is that for this small sliver of time in which we are living, He wants to use it to help determine our usefulness to Him throughout eternity. Our commitment to God's Word on this earth is proportional to our use of money.

II Peter 3:11 says, "Since all these things are to be destroyed in this way, what sort of people ought you to be in holy conduct and godliness."

Attitude About Wealth

What, then, is the correct attitude for the Christian to have towards wealth? To seek *God's* purpose for what is supplied to him.

It is important for the Christian to trust God in *every* circumstance. If we believe that God really loves us and will give us only that amount of money that we can handle without worry, we can have perfect peace in finances. But not until we have committed our *entire* resource to Him.

It becomes clear that money is a training ground for God to develop (and for us to discover) our trustworthiness. "If therefore you have not been faithful in the use of unrighteous Mammon, who will entrust the true riches to you?" (Luke 16:11).

Why do Christians have difficulty trusting God in this area? We really don't believe that He will only do the *best* for us. So we have the tendency to want to withhold a part of what we have. But until a Christian has experienced freedom in the area of money, he will *never* experience God's total plan for his life.

Folklore

In order to dispel some of the old religious folklore that exists concerning this area of money, let's take a look at each myth and then discuss what attitude God wants us to have.

1. An old folklore suggests that *poverty is next to spirituality. Wrong!* There is no inherent virtue in poverty. There are dishonest poor just as there are dishonest rich. Look through Scripture; God never impoverished anyone *because* of his spirituality. Even in Job's case, although God allowed his wealth to be removed, it was as a testimony to Him, and when Job stood true to God, He returned his wealth two-fold. God never once in Scripture relates spirituality to poverty. Therefore, there is no way that any Christian can attain spirituality by impoverishing himself or his family.

God condemns the *misuse* or the *preoccupation* with money, *not* the money itself. In Scripture, God lists the production of money as a spiritual gift. Romans 12:5-8 describes the gift of giving. Obviously, if there is a gift of giving, there must be a gift of gathering, as it is impossible to give otherwise. In *every* scriptural reference, God promises that as we give, so it will be given back to us.

2. *Money brings happiness* is another folklore that is completely false. There is no relationship between money and happiness. "Instruct those who are rich in this present world not to be conceited or to fix their hope on the uncertainty of riches, but on God, who richly supplies

us with all things to enjoy" (I Timothy 6:17). If riches could bring happiness, then the wealthy of the earth ought to be the most content. But, instead, we find many frustrated wealthy people. They have anxieties over what they are going to do with their money, how they are going to leave it to their children, and what effect it will have. And few children are appreciative of the large amounts of wealth their families' leave them. Most, having grown up in affluence, see the devastating effect that an excess of money used unwisely can have on a family.

3. *To be wealthy is a sin.* That's folklore, too. Having money is *not* a sin. As a matter of fact, many times when God finds someone with the proper *attitude,* He blesses them with great riches. When God bestowed riches on Abraham, it was not His intention to corrupt the nation of Israel. And when Solomon prayed for wisdom to be able to manage the people of Israel, God responded by granting him wisdom *and* great wealth. Psalms 8:6 says, "Thou dost make him to rule over the works of Thy hands." This is God's stewardship to us over *everything* on earth.

4. *Money is the root of all evil.* Not so. Many people believe this misquote comes from Scripture. They say, "I don't know exactly where, but the Bible says that money is the root of all evil." That is *not* what the Bible says at all. Paul points out in I Timothy 6:10, "For the *love* of money is a root of all sorts of evil, and some by longing for it have wandered away from the faith, and pierced themselves with many a pang." This is God's perspective; the *love* of money is the root of all sorts of evil.

Christ relates this attitude to the rich young ruler. He came before Jesus and asked Him, " 'Good Teacher, what shall I do to obtain eternal life?' Jesus said to him, 'Why do you call Me good? No one is good except God alone. You know the commandments, "Do not commit adultery, do not murder, do not steal, do not bear false witness, honor your father and mother." ' And he said, 'All these things I have kept from my youth.' And when Jesus heard this, He said to him, 'One thing you still lack; sell all that you possess, and distribute it to the poor, and you shall have treasure in heaven; and come, follow Me' " (Luke 18:18-22).

That young man turned sadly and went away, for he was very rich. And Christ said, "How hard it is for those who are wealthy to enter the kingdom of God!" (Luke 18:24). Why was this? Christ knew that *inside* this man loved his money. He had kept all the external commandments, but he could not keep that internal *attitude* straight. Because of this, Christ asked him to sell what he had and follow Him. He refused to do so, yet, in death, he surrendered what in life he could not.

Attitude is always God's concern. Christ's statement dealing with the rich young ruler was based on that man's attitude, his motivation and the purpose behind his money.

How Is God's Will Expressed in Finances?

The key to Christians realizing God's will in the area of finances is a proper understanding of stewardship. Unfortunately, this term has been so misused that today most people think of stewardship only in terms of Christian fund-raising activities. As defined earlier, a steward is one who manages another's property. We are merely stewards of God's property while we are on this earth, and God can choose to entrust us with as much or as little as He desires. But in no case do we ever actually take *ownership.* When we try to do so we are depending either on what Satan can supply or what we can achieve through our own self-will.

Once a Christian accepts his role as a steward and manages God's resources according to His direction, God will entrust more and more to him. But why would He entrust property to one whom He knows will hoard it and to one who feels he is the owner?

WHAT IS WEALTH?

God will not force His will on us. A Scripture that relates specifically to God's attitude is Proverbs 28:26, "He who trusts in his own heart is a fool, but he who walks wisely, will be delivered." Indeed, God is looking over the entire earth for men who have the proper attitude toward money and who will use it according to His direction and not according to their own self-interest.

Every parable that Christ left us about money tells us many things about the attitude He desires for us to have. The parable of the talents is rich in wisdom (Matthew 25: 14-30, summarized):

The master was going on a trip, and he called in three of his servants, telling them, "I'm taking a long trip and entrusting to you money to use on my behalf." To the first he gave five talents, to the second he gave two talents, and to the third he gave one, each according to his own ability. (Note that he didn't give each the *same*; he gave them according to the physical, worldly ability that they possessed.)

Immediately, upon the master's leaving, the first took the five talents, invested them and promptly earned five more. The second, who had the two talents, took them out and invested them and promptly earned two more.

But the one to whom one talent had been entrusted, knowing that his master was a harsh man, wrapped it in a handkerchief and buried it in the ground.

Later the master returned and called for his three servants. He spoke to the first saying, "How did you fare?" The first said, "I've done well, Master; I've taken your five and gotten five more talents with them." His master then replied, "Well, done; you were good and faithful with the few things I put you in charge of, and you have entered into my great joy."

Then the one who had the two came up and said, "Master, you gave me two, and I've gained two more with them." The master said, "Very good. You are faithful also. I'll put you in charge of many things."

And the one who had received the one talent came to the master and told him, "Master, I knew you to be a hard man, reaping where you did not sow and gathering where you scattered not seed. I was afraid and I went away and hid your talent in the ground. Here, I'll return it to you." But his master told him, "You are a wicked and lazy slave. You knew that I would reap where I did not sow and gather where I scattered no seed. You should have put my money in the bank and at least earned interest on it." He told those around him, "Take the talent from the one who has invested poorly and give it to the one who had five. Because to every one who has shall more be given, and he shall have abundance. But from the one who does not have, even what he does have will be taken away, and cast him out into the darkness."

This parable is *prophetic* in nature. It is given in the 25th chapter of Matthew, a chapter that deals with the second coming of Christ. It reveals many things:

1. God will entrust to us that which is within our own ability and not beyond it.

2. God is the owner and has the right to recover what He has given us to manage.

3. God thoroughly disapproves of slothfulness on our part and expects multiplication of the assets He leaves us, not just maintenance. That multiplication is to be achieved according to *ability.*

God expects those who have the ability to invest, but He also expects the return of what is given. This involves *wisdom* in finances—another key to understanding God's plan.

WHAT IS WEALTH?

God's Wisdom in Money

How can we seek God's wisdom in this area of Christian finances? We must thoroughly understand that God's will is not always coincidental with ours. God says that if we pray anything in His will, believing, it shall be given to us. But God's will and His ways are not always ours. So when we turn our finances over to God, we must also be willing to accept His direction.

Too often we strike out on our own without any clear direction, sometimes borrowing money to do His work. We forget God says He will not frustrate His work for the lack of money.

There is nothing wrong with asking God's direction. But it is wrong to strike out on our own, without direction from God, expecting Him to bail us out. Christians who do this regularly have not really accepted that God's wisdom is superior to theirs.

How God Works Through Our Finances

1. *God will use money in our lives to strengthen our trust in Him.* It is often through money that God can clearly and objectively show us that He *is* God and in control of everything. Matthew 6:32,33: "For all these things the Gentiles eagerly seek; for your heavenly Father knows that you need all these things. But seek first His kingdom and His righteousness; and all these things shall be added to you." This principle establishes that God will use money to strengthen our trust if we will just accept our positions as stewards and turn it over to Him.

2. *God will use money to develop our trustworthiness.* This principle is important because our lives revolve around the making, spending, saving and other uses of

54

money. God will use this area to develop trustworthiness in us. Luke 16:11 states: "If therefore you have not been faithful in the use of unrighteous Mammon, who will entrust the true riches to you?"

3.   *God will use money in a Christian's life to prove His love.* Many Christians remain outside God's will because they are afraid to yield their lives and their resources to Him. Matthew 7:11 has the answer: "If you then, being evil, know how to give good gifts to your children, how much more shall your Father who is in heaven give what is good to those who ask Him!" By this Scripture, we can see God assumes the responsibility of providing the basic necessities for everyone trusting Him.

4.   *God will use money in our lives to demonstrate His power over this world.* Too often we forget that we worship the creator of the universe. We think of God in human terms and relate to Him as we relate to a human. It is important that we understand God's power and His resources.

A story may help to explain this principle. Let's say that one day you're in your home and a man knocks on the door. As you answer the door, he says, "Sir, I've decided that I'm going to give you $1,000 in two weeks." He then leaves you his card and shuts the door. You think, "How strange that was," but the first thing you do is start checking him out. You want to find out what his bank balance is, and how much money he is worth. You begin to talk to people around you who might know something about him.

You discover that he is a multi-billionaire and that he has given thousands of dollars to other people. Knowing this, your confidence in him grows. But still, you don't have any real trust in him because he has not given *you* any money. However, in two weeks he returns and delivers the $1,000. Your trust in him grows more. But, even while you are rejoicing in your great luck and good fortune, you still have some questions. Then, in another two weeks, he returns and says, "Sir, I've decided to give you $10,000 in two more weeks." You already know that he is a multi-billionaire so you know that he has the resources. Then, in talking to other people, you discover that, sure enough, he has given away tens of thousands of dollars as well. This time, you discover something else: He never lies under any circumstances. When he says that he's going to do something, he always does it. In fact, he has put his money into trust and the trust will pay out simply on his word.

In two weeks, he returns and delivers to you the $10,000. Now your trust really grows. Over the next few months, he continues to give you more and more money; each time your trust in him grows.

Then one time he comes to you, after having departed for awhile, and says, "In three months, I will give you $100,000." Well, by this time you have absolute confidence in him. You know exactly how he operates. You know that he has the funds and you know that he has put them in a trust; and once he says it, it will be done. You also know that he has given hundreds of thousands of dollars to other people as well. And so, with full confidence, you can actually spend that money, knowing that he's going to deliver exactly what he said.

Trust in God is very similar. When God promises us things, He promises them through His Word. And the Bible has in it everything that God will ever do for us. As we read it, we begin to understand that God indeed is the owner of everything. He is a *multi-zillionaire*, He is a *multi-universaire,* and when He *says* He can supply things, He can. In talking to others, we find that, what God promises in Scripture He delivers.

He then begins to give—small things at first, because we are only capable of trusting Him for small things. But as He gives us small things, our confidence begins to grow; and the more our confidence in Him grows, the more He is able to supply. Thus God can use money to demonstrate His power to us. "For the Scripture says, 'Whoever believes in Him will never be disappointed.' For there is no distinction between Jew and Greek; for the same Lord is Lord of all, abounding in riches for all who call upon Him" (Romans 10: 11,12).

5. *God will use money to unite Christians through many shared blessings.* "He who gathered much did not have too much, and he who gathered little had no lack" (II Corinthians 8:15). God will use the abundance of one Christian to supply the needs of another. Later He may reverse the relationship, as described in II Corinthians 8:14: "At this present time your abundance being a supply for their want, that their abundance also may become a supply for your want, that there may be equality." It is important, as we are facing these times of economic chaos, that Christians accept the principle that a surplus of money in our lives, indeed everything that we have, is there for a purpose.

For example, God sent Joseph into Egypt specifically to supply the needs of Israel. Had Joseph refused his position of stewardship, God would have simply assigned it to someone else.

6. *God uses money to provide direction for our lives.* There is probably no way that God can direct our lives faster than through the abundance or lack of money. Too often today we believe God will direct our lives only through the abundance of money, and we keep probing around to see where He supplies the money. However, through the lack of money, God will steer us down His path just as quickly. "And let us not lose heart in doing good, for in due time we shall reap if we do not grow weary" (Galatians 6:9). This Scripture tells us that we don't give up just because we face some difficulty. God will ultimately supply the direction that we are seeking, and one of the primary ways that He gives insight into His will is by providing or withholding money. A Christian seeking God's will must be certain that he has first re-

linquished control of his life, including his finances, and is truly seeking God's direction.

7. *God can also use money to satisfy the needs of others.* Christians who hoard their money and how never have any plan for their financial lives, cannot experience this area of fulfillment. Often I hear Christians say, "How can I give? I only have enough to barely meet my needs now." If we have never learned to give, God can never give back, because God cannot be in control so long as we believe we are the owners.

Attitudes of Self-control

Now, let's look at some guides that will clearly define when God is *not* in control, for understanding that is just as important as understanding when He *is* in control.

1. *God will never use money in a Christian's life to worry him.* If a Christian is worried, frustrated and upset about money, it is an absolute certainty that God is *not* in control. Remember, God said that wealth without worry is His plan for our lives. If we are worried and upset over the abundance or the lack of money, God is *not* managing our affairs. "For this reason I say to you, do not be anxious for your life, as to what you eat, or what you shall drink; nor for your body, as to what you shall put on. Is not life more than food, and the body more than clothing?" (Matthew 6:25). This Scripture tells us not to be anxious and upset or worried and frustrated over money. If we are operating within His plan, God promises to supply food, clothing and shelter, the *needs* of life. Believing this, we can concentrate on other things, using the ability that God has given us to accomplish the plan He has for our lives.

2. *God will never use money in the life of a Christian to corrupt him.* Now this seems almost ridiculous on the

surface; naturally, God would not use money to corrupt us. But many Christians have fallen into Satan's trap and are being corrupted. They fail to realize this principle; *God cannot be in control when they are becoming corrupted.* "For the Lord knows the ways of the righteous, but the way of the wicked will perish" (Psalms 1:6). A Christian whose financial life is characterized by greed, ego, deceit or any of the many other worldly snares is not God's ally.

3.　*God will never use money in the life of a Christian to build his ego.* Frequently, Christians are trapped by financial ego. Most people cater to the wealthy in our country (Christians included). Too often in our churches the deacons are selected by their wealth or position rather than by their spiritual commitment to the Lord. It is important that we understand, God will *not* use money to build our egos. Read through the book of James. It makes very clear the admonition not to fawn over the wealthy. We are not to give special privileges because of wealth, but to treat each man as equal to the other.

In Christ we are all financially equal. The things of this world will quickly pass away. Death will remove all wealth from us. And, when we as Christians meet again, there are going to be many surprises. Those who will have the crowns of heaven and are placed in charge of the cities of God will not be those using money to build egos. "And let the rich man glory in his humiliation, because like flowering grass he will pass away. For the sun rises with a scorching wind, and withers the grass; and its flower falls off, and the beauty of its appearance is destroyed; so too the rich man in the midst of his pursuits will fade away " (James 1:10,11).

4.　*God will not allow Christians to hoard money.* There is a distinct difference between saving and hoarding. Solomon said (in paraphrase), "Lord, I ask but two things from You: first, help me to never tell a lie; second, give to me neither riches nor poverty because in my poverty, I might steal, and in my riches I might become content without You." The wealthy have a great responsibility to understand why God gave them money and to avoid hoarding.

I believe that as the economy crumbles, it will not be possible to hoard. Those who have been storing up wealth in contemplation of things unknown, retirement, the better life, or whatever, will be greatly disappointed when it is all consumed like so much chaff and fodder.

A Christian *cannot* be within God's will and hoard money. "For he sees that even wise men die; the stupid and the senseless alike perish, and leave their wealth to others. Their inner thought is, that their houses are forever, and their dwelling places to all generations; they have called their lands after their own names" (Psalms 49:10,11). This is an important spiritual lesson.

Those who hoard large sums of money to leave to their children or hoard large sums of money for "security" are fooling themselves. It cannot be done. It is important that Christians understand and believe this. Scripture speaks very strongly about true values: "I advise you to buy from Me gold refined by fire, that you may become rich, and white garments, that you may clothe yourself, and that the shame of your nakedness may not be revealed, and eyesalve to annoint your eyes, that you may see" (Revelation 3:18).

Hoarding can evolve into a trap. It is possible to see others in need and ignore them rather than abandon a hoarding plan. Unfortunately, those trapped by hoarding can rationalize their behavior by at least a thousand arguments, none of which hold water in light of God's Word

5. *God will not use money to allow us to satisfy our every whim and desire.* It is important also that we begin to adjust to lifestyles compatible with a Christian commitment. This means something less than lavishness. God does not want us to live in poverty; we have discovered that there is nothing inherently spiritual in poverty. Neither

is there any sin in wealth. However, God does not desire for a Christian to live in worldly lavishness while His work needs money and other Christians go without food and clothing. So, while we can live well—and in this country we live very well—it is important that there be a difference in our commitment as compared to that of the non-believer.

What kind of commitment is it to be? It must be one for *you* personally, brought on by a conviction of the Holy Spirit. But you must ask yourself, "Is there a difference between my lifestyle and the non-believer's?" If not, you need to seek God's direction. I Timothy 6:6-8 says, "But godliness actually is a means for great gain, when accompanied by contentment. For we have brought nothing into the world, so we cannot take anything out of it either. And if we have food and covering, with these things we shall be content."

Christians should understand that God does not supply money to satisfy our every whim and desire. His promise is to meet our needs and provide an abundance so that we can help other people. It is when we accept this principle that God will multiply our abundance as well.

Application

To achieve God's best, we must *apply* what He says. In order for this study to be useful to you, you must *apply* the principles that God's Word teaches. Information without application leads to frustration. A Christian who is not experiencing the peace and fulfillment in financial matters that the Bible promises is in bondage. In the next section, we are going to discuss exactly that—financial bondage from God's perspective.

CHAPTER SEVEN

WHAT IS FINANCIAL BONDAGE?

What is financial bondage? As we look in Scripture, it becomes obvious that excessive debts meant exactly that —bondage. If a debtor could not repay his obligations, then the lender had the right to imprison him until he could pay up every cent. The lender then owned everything that had once belonged to that individual—his wife, his family, all of his possessions.

Physical Bondage

The biblical perspective of bondage is expressed in Matthew 5:25,26: "Make friends quickly with your opponent at law while you are with him on the way; in order that your opponent may not deliver you to the judge, and the judge to the officer, and you be thrown into prison. Truly I say to you, you shall not come out of there, until you have paid up the last cent." So it is obvious that in the Bible financial bondage means physical bondage.

This harsh treatment was meted out because the failure to repay a debt was equated with dishonesty. Dishonesty was so frowned upon that usually when a thief was caught, his hand was cut off as a punishment for his crime. Someone who failed to repay an obligation was thrown into prison for the rest of his life and sold as a slave. Why? A man's word was his mark of honor. When one gave his word, he was expected to keep it and anyone who failed to do so could no longer be trusted. Today, society has become too sophisticated to incarcerate someone simply because of debts. Unfortunately, a new punishment has supplanted the old one.

Mental Bondage

Physical bondage has been replaced by *mental bondage.* Every year, thousands upon thousands of families are destroyed because of financial bondage. Thousands, perhaps millions, of people encumber themselves with debts beyond their ability to repay. Christians become involved in the world system just as non-Christians do and begin to purchase on impulse. Credit cards have supplied the means of buying on impulse, allowing virtually anyone to encumber himself far beyond his ability to repay.

Danger of Borrowing

Why do Christians fall trap to this system? Because they have violated one or more scriptural principles that God laid down, particularly those relating to financial bondage. It is important that a Christian understand God's attitude about *debt.* Proverbs 22:7 says, "The rich rules over the poor, and the borrower becomes the lender's slave." God says that when someone borrows, he becomes a *servant* of the lender; the lender is established as an *authority* over the borrower. This should clearly define God's attitude about borrowing from secular sources to do His work. After all, how many Christian organizations would like to be the servant of a secular banking or financial institution?

Christians can get into financial bondage from either of two positions.

Credit Bondage

First, and most common by far, is excessive use of credit or debt. Many individuals today think the credit card companies will not allow them to borrow beyond their ability to repay, but such is *not* the case. The average credit card company in the United States will allow an individual to borrow 250% more than he can conceivably repay.

Delinquent accounts are generally regulated by statutes favoring the creditor, meaning that *delinquent debts* fall under a different set of rules. These rules allow the creditors to charge more interest for debts in delinquency than they can for accounts that are current.

Debt

The scriptural definition of a debt is the inability to meet obligations agreed upon. In other words, when a person buys something on credit terms, that is not necessarily a debt, it is a contract. But, when the terms of that contract are violated, scriptural debt occurs.

The fact that someone is in debt is the result of an earlier *attitude*—that of not understanding or obeying God's principles. "And He said to them, 'Beware, and be on your guard against every form of greed; for not even when one has an abundance does his life consist of his possessions' " (Luke 12:15). When a Christian continues to borrow without the means to repay, his attitude falls into the category of deceit and greed. This mindset will surely separate any Christian from God's will.

WHAT IS FINANCIAL BONDAGE?

Many Christians today are shackled by excessive debts, and misuse of finances has ruined their spiritual lives. They are no longer able to minister to people as God directs; they feel encumbered and have a timidity in speaking about Christ. They are also defeated in their homes, harassed by their spouses and frustrated or intimidated by creditors constantly bearing down on them.

Proverbs 21:17 says, "He who loves pleasure will become a poor man: he who loves wine and oil will not become rich." In other words, one who is never willing to sacrifice, never willing to deny his impulses, but constantly seeks to indulge his whimsical desires, will always be in bondage and frustrated. Until a Christian has brought his debts under control according to God's plan, no peace will *ever* be realized. Remember, God is concerned with *attitude;* He will begin to work in a Christian's finances, regardless of past actions, as soon as the attitude is correct.

No Allowance for Avoiding Creditors

There may be legal remedies to avoid creditors, such as bankruptcy, but there are no such scriptural remedies. "The wicked borrows and does not pay back, but the righteous is gracious and gives" (Psalms 37:21).

In worldly terms, this principle will not seem logical. To the unsaved, it will seem utter nonsense. Many times even Christians begin to doubt God, often saying, "How will I live if they take everything?"

Thus we begin to seek "logical" ways to shelter possessions from legitimate creditors. But as Christians we cannot do that. We must accept the fact that God is in control and that He understands our needs and promises to provide them.

Attitude is the key, for it is attitude that brings into play a source of supernatural power. God says, "If you ask Me anything in My name, I will do it" (John 14:14).

So we must accept God's plan of recovery when in financial bondage.

God's Promise

If we really trust God with everything that we have, He will satisfy all of our needs as He promised. "For all these things the nations of the world eagerly seek; but your Father knows that you need these things. But seek for His kingdom, and all these things shall be added to you" (Luke 12:30, 31).

One of the greatest scriptural references to attitude can be found in the story of Abraham. God asked Abraham to sacrifice his most important possession—his son Isaac. Born of his old age, Abraham truly loved his son, and, although Abraham was a wealthy man by worldly standards, nothing meant as much to him as Isaac.

But God asked Abraham to take his son up to the mountains and sacrifice him unto the Lord. He asked Abraham, as He asks us, to sacrifice everything for His name's sake. Abraham could have argued with God concerning the logic of sacrificing Isaac, but he did not. Abraham knew that if God had given him a son in his old age, surely God could recover him from death.

So he packed up the mules, his servants and Isaac, and set out for the mountain. Laying his son upon the altar, Abraham raised the knife.

It was at that point that God stopped him, saying, "Abraham, I know that you are a true man and you have withheld nothing. Because you withheld nothing, I'll make your seed as abundant as the sand upon the shore. And I'll bless you beyond every nation on earth" (Genesis 22:16,17, paraphrased).

As a result of Abraham's obedience, God entrusted to him stewardship of His kingdom on this earth. For not only did Abraham love and trust God, but he bowed his will to God's judgment. Christians must accept this concept of total stewardship, because when they transfer assets to avoid creditors, when they file bankruptcy to avoid creditors, or when they deal deceitfully with creditors, God's channel for help is blocked.

Bondage Through Wealth

Financial bondage can also exist through an *abundance* of money. Some Christians have been supplied a surplus of money and have misused or begun to hoard it. Those who use their money totally for self-satisfaction or hoard it away for that elusive "rainy day" are just as financially bound in God's eyes as those in debt.

The accumulation of wealth and material pleasures of life can be an obsession that will destroy a Christian's health, destroy his family, separate him from friends and block God's will in his life. Everything and everybody can become objects to be used on the ladder to success. Those shackled by these wrong attitudes are always striving for the goal of money. Job 31: 24-28 says: "If I have put my confidence in gold, and called fine gold my trust, if I have gloated because my wealth was great, and because my hand had secured so much; if I have looked at the sun when it shone, or the moon going in splendor, and my heart became secretly enticed, and my hand threw a kiss from my mouth, that too would have been an iniquity calling for judgment, for I would have denied God above."

As discussed earlier, it is important for Christians to understand this truth. Many Christians have taken the very resource that God provided for their peace and comfort and transformed it into something full of pain and sorrow. There is nothing inherently evil in money itself, only the preoccupation and the misuse of it.

WHAT IS FINANCIAL BONDAGE?

Symptoms of Bondage

It is important to be able to recognize and detect the *symptoms* of financial bondage. How can you tell when financial bondage occurs? If any of the following conditions exist:

1. Overdue Bills.

A Christian is in financial bondage when he experiences anxiety produced from overdue bills. In counseling, I find that as high as 80% of Christian families today either presently suffer from overspending or have suffered from this malady in the past. This is due in part because most families have no plan for their finances and continue to borrow beyond their ability to repay.

If a Christian is shackled in this area, it is virtually impossible to be an effective witness for Jesus Christ. Frustration created in the home life will be reflected in the spiritual life. Proverbs 27:12 says, "A prudent man sees evil and hides himself, the naive proceed and pay the penalty." God is saying through this proverb that a man who is prudent or plans well will foresee dangers and avoid them, but the foolish man will just rush in, do whatever is convenient at the time, and then will end up paying the penalty later.

2. Investment Worries.

Worrying over investments, savings, money or assets also causes financial bondage and interferes with the Christian's spiritual life. This is the case with many Christians. As they begin to accumulate material goods (or worry about not accumulating them), worry is carried over to every aspect of their lives. Many Christians never enjoy their families because of concern over investments or the lack of investments. This worry follows them home, to church, even to bed. They go to bed with money on their minds and wake up to the same thoughts.

If these investments generate worry, a Christian can be absolutely sure that he is not within God's will. "No one

68

can serve two masters; for either he will hate the one and love the other, or he will hold to the one and despise the other. You cannot serve God and Mammon. For this reason I say to you, do not be anxious for your life, as to what you shall eat, or what you shall drink; nor for your body, as to what you shall put on. Is not life more than food, and the body than clothing?" (Matthew 6:24, 25).

3. "Get Rich Quick" Attitude.

This attitude is characterized by attempts to make money quickly with very little applied effort. An investment is a "get rich quick" program if an individual must assume excessive debt, borrow the money to invest, or deal deceitfully with people.

Proverbs says that a man who wants to get rich fast will quickly fail. "A faithful man will abound with blessings, but he who makes haste to be rich will not go unpunished" (Proverbs 28:20). Money that may have taken years of effort to accumulate can be lost in days in a get rich quick program.

Proverbs 28:22 says, "A man with an evil eye hastens after wealth, and does not know that want will come upon him." This typifies someone who does not desire to put any effort in his gain. A Christian should make no provision in his plans for such schemes.

Not only is this get rich quick attitude prevalent in investments, but it also surfaces in the home when a family borrows to get everything desired rather than saving for the items. It's important to assess exactly what your *motives* are for financial involvement.

4. No Gainful Employment.

Financial bondage also exists when there is no desire for gainful employment. Paul said in II Thessalonians 3:10, "For even when we were with you, we used to give you this order: If anyone will not work, neither let him eat."

Unfortunately, in our society today, we have lost this point of reference. The government has assumed responsibility to support those deserving and non-deserving. This area must also be assessed in every Christian's life. For many people who desire "to start at the top" never get started at all. Each of us must have a real desire for gainful employment if we are to accomplish what God put us on this earth to do.

Also, every Christian should ask himself, when approached for assistance, "Am I asked to supply others needs, wants or desires? Does this individual really have an internal commitment for gainful employment?" It is possible to keep someone from God's perfect plan for them by satisfying their requests.

Paul is a good example of the kind of attitude we should have. He worked throughout his Christian life. But Paul found through his travels there were many Christians who had no real desire for gainful employment. These relied on the brethren to take care of them. Paul admonished these people, particularly those in the church at Thessalonica, and he reminded those who did work that it was not their responsibility to support those who did not. "Now we command you, brethren, in the name of our Lord Jesus Christ, that you keep aloof from every brother who leads an unruly life and not according to the tradition which you received from us" (II Thessalonians 3:6).

5. *Deceitfulness*.

A Christian is in financial bondage if his basic attitude includes dishonesty with others in financial matters.

It is important that each Christian assess his own life concerning this attitude. Have you dealt completely honestly and openly with everyone? In the worldly way, this will not seem logical many times. For instance, someone selling insurance or investments can easily shade the truth (rather than telling the whole truth, tell only *part* of the truth). To do so is deceitful and will financially bind a Christian, removing peace and contentment.

Christian families must make a similar assessment. This bondage can occur, for instance, if a couple purchases an appliance on credit, knowing that they are already behind in their average monthly obligations. They are dealing deceitfully with the supplier. "Better is a poor man who walks in his integrity than he who is perverse in speech and is a fool" (Proverbs 19:1)

You will recall that Luke 16:10 relates God's attitude toward deceit: "He who is faithful in a very little thing is faithful also in much; and he who is unrighteous in a very little thing is unrighteous also in much." This principle is true in each and every one of our lives. If we are not faithful in small things, we are *not* going to be faithful in large things. The amount is not important.

6. Greediness.

Financial bondage will also result from an attitude of greediness. This attitude is reflected when someone always wants the best or always wants more than he has. Someone who is never able to put others first, never able to accept a loss when it's necessary or is always looking at what others have suffers from greed. A Christian who cannot put his own *wants* and *desires* behind him to satisfy the *needs* of others suffers from greed. "For this you know with certainty, that no immoral or impure person or covetous man, who is an idolater, has an inheritance in the kingdom of Christ and God" (Ephesians 5:5). What is an idolater? It is one who puts material possessions before God. We are often guilty of establishing other idols before God.

The rich ruler we reviewed in Luke 18 suffered from this malady. He had put an idol, his money, before God, and he could not give up that idol, even to follow Christ.

7. Covetousness.

Financial bondage exists if the Christian's attitude is one of looking at what others have and desiring it. In our society, we might call this "keeping up with the Joneses." "Look at what the Joneses have; why can't we have that too?"

I often hear young married couples' discussions about

how they got started on the road to indebtedness. They simply followed the example of other people who borrowed to get the things they wanted—furniture, new cars, televisions and such. They decided, "Why can't we get the same things they do by borrowing?"

It's sad that they can't look *inside* the Joneses' house. They need to observe what kind of strife takes place when the paycheck comes in and there's never enough to satisfy all the creditors. Or the anxiety that takes place when a notice comes from a collection agency taking them to court. Or the despair of a housewife when a creditor calls at 10 a.m. asking for his money.

Covetousness is not limited to this present generation either: "But as for me, my feet came close to stumbling; my steps had almost slipped. For I was envious of the arrogant, as I saw the prosperity of the wicked" (Psalms 73:2,3).

This attitude should not characterize the Christian. Set your goals and standards based on God's conviction—not on what others have. *Peace and contentment* are worth anything. I am positive that virtually any couple in bondage would willingly go back to zero with no assets and no liabilities if they could do so.

8. *Family Needs Unmet.*

A Christian is in financial bondage if, because of his past buying habits, his family needs cannot be met. The reasons for unmet needs can be numerous: a Christian may refuse gainful employment; he may be shackled with debts to the point that creditors take necessary family funds; the stan-

dard of living may be such that "luxuries" deprive the family of "needs." This is not as uncommon as one might think because many Christians live far beyond their means and sacrifice basic necessities such as medical or dental care as a result.

The "symptoms" for this bondage are almost inexhaustible but are all related to a common attitude—*irresponsibility*. There is a definite difference between a Christian who is financially bound because of irresponsibility and one who cannot meet family needs because of the circumstances surrounding him—such as medical bills, injury, illness or other unforeseeable events. In these instances, it is the responsibility of other Christians to help satisfy the family needs.

The financial bondage discussed here concerns those who are wanting because of past bad habits and those who will not meet the needs of their families. Paul said in I Timothy 5:8, "But if any one who does not provide for his own, and especially for those in his household, he has denied the faith, and is worse than an unbeliever." No Christian can achieve God's will in his life until the attitude that caused this bondage is changed.

9 Unmet Christian Needs.

Unfortunately, this is the norm in our society today. But it is the responsibility of each and every Christian to supply the *needs* of others who *cannot* do so for themselves.

James 2:15,16 relates that same thinking: "If a brother or sister is without clothing and in need of daily food, and one of you says to them, 'Go in peace, be warmed and be filled'; and yet you do not give them what is necessary for their body; what use is that?"

Harry Truman once said of the presidency, "The buck stops here." The same is true for each Christian. If we see a brother or a sister going without, and we close our hearts to them, what kind of love is that? Of course, God will not lay *every* need on *every* Christian's heart, but He will lay on our hearts specific needs that we are to meet. And if we pass them by, He must simply seek out someone else to share in the blessing.

It is as Mordecai told Esther, "And who knows whether you have not attained royalty for such a time as this?" (Esther 4:14b). A similar question can be asked for every Christian. Who knows but that God has given us money for that specific time when we see a brother in need?

10. *Overcommitment to Work.*

A life that is devoted to business pursuits, to the exclusion of all else, is a life of bondage. Not only are many Christians worried and frustrated about investments, but their lives are dominated by work; everywhere they go their work follows them and every discussion is centered around their business. But God's plan for work is to *excel,* not *exceed.*

11. *Money Entanglements.*

God says a Christian is in financial bondage when his money entanglements reduce his Christian effectiveness. Entanglements differ from overcommitment to work in that they stem from a mishandling of finances, perhaps even deceitfully. Often this bondage is described as "too many irons in the fire."

Someone trapped by entanglements is so "strung out" that he has to continually apply "band aids" to his financial ventures. These entanglements become so complex that continual manipulation is required to keep the whole mess from collapsing. Often someone in this situation has dealt with so many people unfairly that he can no longer be an effective witness for Christ, and many times he has also involved other friends in these ventures. As others lose confidence in his integrity, that reduces his Christian effectiveness even further.

Once people know that a Christian deals questionably or that he is in constant financial bondage, his personal witness and family relationship collapse. What does he have that other people might want? How is his life different from that of a non-Christian? "For if after they have escaped the defilements of the world by the knowledge of the Lord and Savior Jesus Christ, they are again entangled in them and are overcome, the last state has become worse for them than the first" (II Peter 2: 20). In other words, once someone understands God's plan for finances and becomes entangled in the world again, the results are worse.

Remember the parable of the sower? Some of the seed fell among the thorns and these thorns were the pressures of life and the riches of life. As they grew up they choked out God's Word. A Christian can understand God's Word and be willing to do it, but the pressures and riches of life can envelope him and choke out God's Word so that he can no longer respond.

12. Financial Unfairness.

God says a Christain is in financial bondage if he deals unfairly with others. In other words, this is a person who promotes his own interests to the detriment of others. A classic example of this kind of bondage is the Christian who discovers someone in need and takes unfair advantage of the situation. He may apply so much pressure that the needy person is forced to accept a poor offer, or even worse, is forced to borrow from the high-pressure Christian.

This tactic is often used in dealing with recent widows or applying pressure sales tactics through church-related contacts. Widows are besieged by "Christian" wolves who attempt to sell them things that they don't need or encourage them to make investments under duress when

they are in a very vulnerable state.

Many people use religious contacts as a means to solicit business—approaching others at church and applying pressure because of Christian involvement. Christians (particularly young couples) often over-buy life insurance or similar services from an older individual who is usually a leader in the church. Pressure is applied on the basis of church involvement rather than the value of what is offered.

But God warns those caught up in this attitude that "income from exploiting the poor will end up in the hands of someone who pities them " (Proverbs 28:8, LB).

This individual is never able to deny himself a material desire but satisfies every whim that comes to mind. "And He was saying to them all, 'If anyone wishes to come after Me, let him deny himself, and take up his cross daily, and follow Me' " (Luke 9:23).

God promises to satisfy every *need* that we have, not every desire. To continually satisfy virtually every whim and desire that comes to our minds moves us outside of God's will. A self-indulger can be identified by one or more of the following signs:

1. Purchasing without regard for utility.
2. Living a lifestyle characterized by lavishness.
3. Consistently trading cars and appliances for new models.
4. Having closet after closet full of clothes that are seldom or never used.
5. Spending money frivolously on virtually any "sale" item.

14. *Lack of Commitment to God's Work.*

A Christian is in financial bondage if there is no financial commitment to God's work. It is important to accept this principle as basic to Christian financial management. "Honor the Lord from your wealth, and from the first of all your produce; so your barns will be filled with plenty, and your vats will overflow with new wine"

(Proverbs 3:9,10). It is only by honoring the Lord from the first part of our income that God can take control. As stated many times before, we are stewards; God is the *owner*. The tithe that we give to God is a *testimony* of His ownership. The Christian who fails to give a minimum testimony to God never acknowledges that He is the owner.

15. *Financial Superiority.*

This attitude often occurs in those who are blessed with an abundance. But Scripture holds to a different perspective about money. Someone who has wealth should think of it not as an honor or a right, but a *responsibility*. There should be no financial superiority within the Body of Christ. He who has much should share it with those who have little according to God's plan. But most Christians and Christian organizations cater to wealthy individuals, and many wealthy Christians demand special attention.

God's plan for the last days allows no provision for the financially superior. When in need, everyone is equal, and in the last days, no amount of wealth will yield protection. But the Christians who understand God's Word and have planned accordingly will have plenty.

". . .You say, 'I am rich, and have become wealthy, and have need of nothing,' and you do not know that you are wretched and miserable and poor and blind and naked" (Revelation 3:17). Thus, God describes those who profess superiority. Separated from God, no one is wealthy.

16. *Financial Resentment.*

The converse of superiority is a Christian in financial bondage from feelings of resentment because of God's provision. This characterizes someone who thinks that God has not given him what he deserves or desires. Not only does he covet what others have, but he is basically resentful toward God for his station in life. I believe it is a very dangerous thing for a Christian to ask God to give him what he deserves lest He do it!

Assess any feelings of resentment in relation to need rather than desire. We live better than 98% of the rest of the population on the face of this earth.

It is easy to adjust to large homes, two cars, automatic washers and dryers, refrigerators and air conditioners and then to begin to feel resentful because of all the "things" that other people have. Why is this? Have we become no different than the infidel? Are we no different from the Jews who resented God's provision? In our time of plenty, many want to adjust to lavishness.

Do you believe that everything works together to accomplish God's will for your life? Consider John 6:27: "Do not work for the food which perishes but for the food which endures to eternal life, which the Son of Man shall give to you, for on Him the Father, even God, has set His seal." Be fearful of resentful feelings lest you begin to resent even God.

Summary

So we see that financial bondage can exist from a lack of money and overspending, but it can also exist from an abundance of money and not understanding why God gave it to us.

Continuing to adjust the level of spending to exceed our level of income will result in financial bondage; borrowing is the most common way into bondage. Every Christian must understand God's attitude about debts. He discusses little about *what* we buy with borrowed money but describes in depth the requirement to repay.

Common sense should tell us not to borrow for depreciating assets. They are usually worth less than the amount owed and may well fall into what God calls "surety." Surety is putting yourself up as a guarantor for material assets. But it depends on the economy whether a particular item is depreciating or appreciating.

In helping you to determine what God's will for you is in the area of borrowing, as in the other areas we will study, I will present the standards that God has revealed to us through His Word. These standards could be explained in terms of a range of possible responses a Christian could have within God's will. Within that range, God will direct each of us to His perfect will for us.

For borrowing, the one end of the range is expressed in Romans 13:8, "Owe nothing to anyone except to love one another; for he who loves his neighbor has fulfilled the law." So at this end of the range, God describes borrowing in terms of *owing no man.* I know personally in my life and the lives of scores of other Christians, there is no greater sense of freedom than to owe no man a financial obligation.

The other end of the range is found in Psalms 37:21, "The wicked borrows and does not pay back, but the righteous is gracious and gives." Thus, at this end of the range, God accepts nothing less than repayment of every obligation. God requires every Christian to operate somewhere between these two points.

CHAPTER EIGHT

GOD'S PLAN FOR FINANCIAL FREEDOM

What Is Freedom?

It is important for a Christian to be able to recognize financial bondage, but it is equally important to know how to achieve freedom. Financial freedom manifests itself in every aspect of the Christian's life—relief from worry and tension about overdue bills, a clear conscience before God and before other men and the absolute assurance that God is in control of his finances.

This is not to say that a Christian's life will be totally void of any difficulties in the area of finances. Often God will allow the consequences of earlier actions to remain in order to reinforce the lesson; also God does not promise to remove every difficulty. But no matter what circumstances are encountered, God promises peace.

When God manages our finances, we have nothing to worry about. *He* is the master of the universe. It is *His* wisdom that we are seeking. We're still human beings and subject to making a mistake at any moment, for even when we understand God's principles, it is possible to step out of His will, as we all do from time to time. But as soon as we admit the error and let God take control again, we are back under His guidance.

Once a Christian truly accepts and experiences financial

freedom, there will never be a desire to stay outside of God's will. Perfect peace is what is promised and perfect peace is what God delivers.

In our society, there are some who have found financial freedom, but I have never met a non-Christian who had true freedom from worry, anxiety, tension, harassment or bitterness about money. Once someone experiences and *lives* financial freedom (meaning freedom from the bondage of debts, freedom from oppression of others, freedom from envy and covetousness or greed and freedom from resentfulness), that person stands out like a beacon at sea.

Steps to Financial Freedom

How can we achieve financial freedom? What must we do according to God's plan?

1. *Transfer Ownership.*

A Christian must transfer ownership of *every* possession to God. This means money, time, family, material possessions, education, even earning potential for the future. This is *essential* to experience the Spirit-filled life in the area of finances. (Psalms 8:6.)

A Christian must realize that there is absolutely no substitute for this step. If you believe that you are the *owner* of even a single possession, then the events affecting that possession are going to affect your attitude. God will not force His will on us. He will not input His perfect will into our lives unless we *first* surrender our will to Him.

If, however, we make a total transfer of everything to God, *He* will demonstrate His ability. It is important to understand and accept God's conditions for His control (Deuteronomy 5:32,33). God will keep His promise to provide every need we have through physical, material and spiritual means, according to His perfect plan.

It is simple to say, "I make total transfer of everything to God," but not so simple to do. At first, anyone will experience some difficulty in consistently seeking God's will in the area of material things because we are so accustomed to self-management and control. But financial freedom comes from knowing that God is in control.

What a great relief it is to turn our burdens over to *Him*. Then, if something happens to the car, you can say, "Father, I gave this car to You; I've maintained it to the best of my ability, but I don't own it. It belongs to You, so do with it whatever You would like." Then look for the blessing that God has in store as a result of this attitude.

I remember a dear friend of mine once shared with me an experience he had after making a total transfer of everything to God. Only a few months earlier he had paid to have the air conditioning system in his house repaired. Then, one day in the summer, the air conditioner quit again. He began to wonder, "Well, Lord, why did You have this happen? Is it that You want another $500 to be put into that air conditioning system? I just can't believe that's Your will, but if so, I submit to it." Then he said the Lord convicted him, saying, "What were you going to do with the $500?"

Again he puzzled, "Well, Lord, if it is Your will that I spend the money on that air conditioning system, I'll do it. But, Lord, if it's not Your will, then I'll put that $500 into whatever You decide."

Indeed, the Lord did have another plan. A brief survey of the situation showed there was nothing wrong with his air conditioning system—it cost nothing to return it to operation. He then found the purpose for that $500 God had entrusted to him. He had no anxiety, no frustration, no worry associated with the incident because he had transferred total ownership to God. And God, in turn, was simply showing him that He had a specific use for that $500.

2.   *Freedom from Debt.*

A Christian must get out of debt altogether. Again, let me define a scriptural *debt*. Debt exists when any of the following conditions are true:

— Payment is past due for money, goods or services that are owed to other people.

— The total value of unsecured liabilities exceeds total assets. In other words, if you had to cash out at any time, there would be a negative balance on your account.

— Anxiety is produced in the area of financial responsibility, and the family's basic needs are not being met either because of past or present buying practices.

Steps to Getting and Staying Current

A. Written Plan.

A written plan is an absolute *necessity* for the Christian who is in financial bondage. (It is of benefit for everyone else, too.)

Use a written plan of all expenditures and their order of importance. The order of importance is crucial because, as I discussed earlier, we have lost the point of reference between needs, wants and desires. Let's examine the differences between a need, a want and a desire:

— *Needs.* These are the purchases necessary to provide your basic requirements such as food, clothing, a job, home, medical coverage and others. "And if we have food and covering, with these we shall be content" (I Timothy 6:8).

— *Wants.* Wants involve choices about the quality of goods to be used. Dress clothes versus work clothes, steak versus hamburger, a new car versus a used car, etc. I Peter 3:3, 4 gives a point of reference for determining wants in a Christian's

83

life: "And let not your adornment be external only—braiding the hair, and wearing gold jewelry, and putting on dresses; but let it be in the hidden person of the heart, with the imperishable quality of a gentle and quiet spirit, which is precious in the sight of God."

— *Desires.* These are choices according to God's plan which can be made only out of surplus funds after all other obligations have been met.

I John 2:15, 16 says, "Do not love the world, nor the things in the world. If anyone loves the world, the love of the Father is not in him. For all that is in the world, the lust of the flesh and the lust of the eyes and the boastful pride of life, is not from the Father, but is from the world."

The difference between needs, wants and desires can be illustrated this way: we can see in our society today that most people need an automobile. That *need* can be satisfied by a used Volkswagen. The want can be satisfied by a larger car such as an Oldsmobile. And the desire may only be satisfied by a brand new Cadillac.

A parallel would be in the food that we eat. The protein requirement of food can be satisfied by selecting good quality vegetables or hamburger. The want may be steak, and the desire may be satisfied only by eating out every night.

Each of us must assess these levels according to the plan that God has for *our* lives. For instance, if a Christian is in financial bondage and is not able to keep his family's needs met and bills paid, he must assess whether a television set is a need, a want or a desire. He must also assess movies or vacations accordingly. Those who are in debt have no prerogative but to meet their needs and then satisfy the needs of their creditors according to God's plan. Always analyze every expenditure made in terms of these categories.

B. *Living Essentials.*

A Christian in debt must stop any expenditure which is not absolutely essential for living (Proverbs 21:17). Look for services around the home that can be done without outside cost. Also begin to develop some home skills. By utilizing individual skills, you can begin to cut down on some of the expenditures which are not really essential.

It's also important to learn to substitute for items of lower depreciation. For example, when purchasing appliances, select those without so many frills on them; the basic components of most appliances are the same. Learn to utilize an automobile even though you may be bored with it.

What I'm expressing is an attitude of conservatism. Begin to eliminate expenditures which are not *essential*, remembering that many expenditures are assumed to be essential only because of our society. Fifty years ago almost all the labor supplied in the home was through family members—not professionals who charged for it. Christians who are in bondage *must* begin to assess what things they  can do for themselves and stop the frivolities. Once a Christian has begun to do these things, whether in debt or not, it will become fun and will help stabilize the family life.

C. *Think Before Buying.*

A Christian who is in debt (and even those who are not) should *think* before every purchase (Proverbs 24:3). Every purchase should be evaluated as follows:

— Is it a necessity? Have I assessed whether it is a need, a want or a desire?

- Does the purchase reflect my Christian ethics? (For example, *Playboy* does not reflect Christian ethics.) Can I continue to take magazines, encyclopedias or book and record subscriptions while I owe others?
- Is this the very best possible buy I can get or am I purchasing only because I have this credit card?
- Is it a highly depreciative item? Am I buying something that will devaluate quickly? (Swimming pools, boats, sports cars all fall into this category.)
- Does it require costly upkeep? (There are many items that fall within this category — mobile homes, swimming pools, color television sets.)

D. Discontinue Credit Buying.

A Christian in debt should also begin buying on a cash basis only. Often someone in debt, with an asset that can be converted into cash, will ask, "Would it be better to sell this asset and pay off the debts?" That's a normal mistake to make, but it only treats the symptom rather than the problem.

I remember a couple who were in dire financial bondage from credit card debts. They owed over $20,000 and paid in excess of $4,000 a year in interest alone. In our planning, it seemed reasonable for them to sell their home and apply the money to their debts,  which would have paid them off. They did so, but less than a year later they were back in again with about $6,000 in credit card debts and no home this time.

What happened? I had treated a symptom rather than the problem. The problem was an attitude dealing with credit cards. I had their assurance that they would not use the credit cards; but without working out a plan for them to discontinue the use of those cards, they fell right back into the same trap again. As soon as they needed something and lacked the cash to purchase it, out came the card.

The principle to observe is this: If you are in debt from the misuse of credit, stop—*totally stop*—using it. One of the best things to do with credit cards when in debt is to pre-heat the oven to 400 degrees and put them in it. Then mail the cards back to their respective companies and ask them to mail you no more. Include in your letter the plan for paying that credit card debt, and then commit yourself to buying solely on a cash basis.

Once good habits have been developed and the bondage from the misuse of credit cards has been broken, then evaluate the feasibility of converting assets to pay off the debts. In that way you won't simply be treating the symptom. Once someone has overextended his finances, it is necessary to sacrifice some of the wants and desires in life to get current; otherwise, he will continue to borrow and only get deeper into bondage.

E.   Avoid Leverage.

When in debt, avoid the use of what is called "leverage." Leverage is the ability to control a large asset with a relatively small amount of invested capital.

For example, if you bought a piece of property that cost $10,000 and required $1,000 down, that represents a nine to one lever. You have invested 10% of your money and borrowed 90%.

Borrowing money to invest is not a scriptural principle. For when a Christian invests and borrows the money from a bank to do so, the repayment of the bank loan is dependent on the investment making a profit. But if a profit is not made and the investor can't make the payments, he loses the investments and still owes the bank. The result? Financial bondage.

Let me clarify a point on the use of leverage. If the 10% down payment is made out of your own money, and the value of the property secures the other 90%, and if payment could not be met, you would simply give the property back and lose the 10%; that is not a *debt*, it is a contract.

It should be understood that although the practice of leverage itself does not violate a scriptural principle, it can fall into the category of a "get rich quick" scheme if used excessively.

F. *Practice Saving.*

A Christian should practice saving money on a regular basis. This *includes* those who are in debt. Even if it is only $5 a month, develop a discipline of saving.

This does not mean to store up a large amount of money to the sacrifice of creditors, but one of the best habits that a young couple can develop is saving a small amount on a regular basis.

Everyone in our society living above the poverty level has the *capability* to save money, but many fail to do so because they believe that the amount that they can save is so small it's meaningless. Others believe that God frowns upon a Christian saving anything. Neither of these two reasons are scriptural. "There is precious treasure and oil in the dwelling of the wise, but a foolish man swallows it up" (Proverbs 21:20). The common attitude presented in the Bible is to save on a regular basis, and it is important that Christians develop *good* habits to replace *bad* habits.

All told, to get out of debt, a Christian must utilize these points we've just discussed; there is no alternative under God's plan for being debt free.

3. *Establish the Tithe.*

Every Christian should establish the tithe as the *minimum* testimony to God's ownership. As mentioned earlier, how can anyone say that he has given total ownership to God when he has never given testimony to that fact?

It is through sharing that we bring His power in finances into focus. In every case, God wants us to give the *first* part to Him, but He also wants us to pay our creditors. That requires establishing a plan and probably making sacrifices of wants and desires until all debts are current.

You cannot sacrifice God's part—that is not your prerogative as a Christian. "Now this I say, he who sows sparingly shall also reap sparingly; and he who sows bountifully shall also reap bountifully" (II Corinthians 9:6). So what is the key? If a sacrifice is necessary, and it almost always is, do not sacrifice God's or your creditor's share. Choose a portion of your own expenditures to sacrifice.

4. Accept God's Provision.

To obtain financial peace, recognize and accept that God's provision is used to direct each of our lives. Often Christians lose sight of the fact that God's will can be accomplished through a withholding of funds; we think that He can direct us only by an abundance of money. But God does not choose for everyone to live in great abundance. As stated before, this does not imply poverty, but it may mean that God wants us to be more responsive to His day-by-day control.

Each Christian *must* learn to live on what God provides and not under pressure brought on by driving desires for wealth and material things. This necessitates planning lifestyles around the provision that God has supplied—it *can* be done.

How can a Christian actually *apply* this principle and find the level of living God has planned for his life? He can begin putting these attitudes into practice in the following areas:

A. Extra Income.

Often when a family cannot pay its bills, the first thought is, "More money will help." Perhaps the husband takes a second job or the wife goes to work. Before either step is taken, a Christian should assess whether he is living outside God's will for his finances. Is a lack of money the problem or is it a wrong attitude?

Seek the possibility of extra income *only* after correcting buying habits. Quite often, when analyzed on paper, a working mother does not contribute any more actual income. In many cases it costs *more* money, considering the costs of child care, travel and clothing. But the greatest sacrifice is the loss of family guidance from the mother. I believe there is no provision in God's Word for a mother with children to work if she must sacrifice her children's welfare. If there are no children at home, or the children are in school during the day, it should be an individual family decision. But it is necessary to first assess whether you are rationalizing that you cannot live within God's provision.

B.   Ask God First.

Before making any purchase, regardless of the amount, give God the opportunity to provide that item first. Many times we pass by the blessings God has in store for us because, being impulse buyers, we purchase without giving God the opportunity to show us *His* will. God will often manifest Himself by providing our needs from a totally unexpected source.

One of the greatest joys that a Christian can experience is God's faithfulness. Psalms 37:7 says, "Rest in the Lord and wait patiently for Him." Give God an opportunity to provide before you go out and purchase.

Several things a Christian should do before every purchase that is outside his normal budget are:

Pray about purchases. Absolutely no purchase is too large or too small to pray about. How can you know God's will if you never ask Him?

Seek family counsel. Bring the entire family into the petition before God and allow them to share in the blessing of God answering prayer.

Seek God's will. Learn to discern God's will in requests. God is not under any obligation to grant our every wish since often we ask for things that hurt us. It is God's wisdom that we are seeking; not ours. "For who has known the mind of the Lord, or who became His counselor?" (Romans 11:34).

5. *A Clear Conscience.*

A Christian must have a clear conscience regarding past business practices and personal dealings. If you will remember, earlier we discussed dealing unfairly with others through greed or ego. Freedom from these may well require restitution as well as a changed attitude.

Proverbs 28:13 says, "He who conceals his transgressions will not prosper, but he who confesses and forsakes them will find compassion." The New Testament reaffirms this in Matthew 5:24, "Leave your offering there before the altar, and go your way, first be reconciled to your brother, and then come and present your offering."

God is saying, "Don't give anything to the Lord as long as you have transgressed against your brother and you are not willing to make it right."

I recall a friend who had wronged an individual financially before he became a Christian. God convicted him about this and indicated that he should go and make restitution. He contacted this individual, confessed what had been done and offered to make it right. The person refused to forgive and refused to take any money.

For awhile it hurt my friend's ego and pride; until he realized that it was not for the offended person that he had confessed, but for himself. It was not for the loss that restitution was offered, but for his relationship with God. God had forgiven him, and he had done exactly what God had asked. Nothing further was required.

6. *Put Others First.*

A Christian seeking financial freedom must always

be willing to put other people *first*. This does not imply that a Christian has to be a floor mat for others; it simply means that he doesn't profit at the disadvantage of someone else. The key, again, lies in *attitude*.

To avoid financial superiority a Christian must apply the attitude God shows us in His Word: "Do nothing from selfishness or empty conceit, but with humility of mind let each of you regard one another as more important than himself; do not merely look out for your own personal interests, but also for the interests of others" (Philippians 2:3,4). *This* is the attitude God desires in the area of finances. For a Christian "bears all things, believes all things, hopes all things, endures all things" (I Corinthians 13:7).

7.   *Limit Time Involvement.*

A Christian must also limit time devoted to business affairs when family involvement suffers. "Do not weary yourself to gain riches, cease from your consideration of it. When you set your eyes on it, it is gone. For wealth certainly makes itself wings, like an eagle that flies toward the heavens" (Proverbs 23:4,5). Many Christians are trapped in this cycle of overcommitment to business or money pursuits.

Money is not always the prime motive for this overcommitment. Often it is ego, escape, or simply habit that drives a person to such excess. Many people overcommit out of pure habit, not ever questioning what they are doing, why they are earning money, or why God put them on this earth.

Psalms 127:2 says, "It is vain for you to rise up early, to retire late, to eat the bread of painful labors; for He gives to His beloved even in his sleep."

It's important to remember that the priorities God sets for us are very clear and that every Christian seeking God's best must understand them. The *first* priority in a Christian's life is developing his personal relationship with Jesus Christ. Remember, as discussed before, you must understand who God is to be able to trust Him, to be able to ask Him for answers and to expect to get them. Understanding God comes from:

Reading His Word. When situations arise, decisions can be made according to His plan.

Praying. Prayer is communication with God. How else can you discern God's perfect will for your life but to ask Him?

Sharing your relationship with Christ with others. This does not mean a "forced" witness, either.

The *second* priority of a Christian's commitment is to his family, including teaching them from God's Word.

This training requires a commitment to the family unit—and that means a specific time commitment, too. Christ deserves the best part of our day. If you study best in the morning, get up early in the morning and give time to the Lord. Sacrifice if necessary to do so. If you find that your family time together can take place best between eight and nine in the evening, commit that time to God. Turn off the television, have the children do their homework early, and begin to study the Bible together. It is important for the whole family to understand God and pray together. Pray for others in need, too. And have your children become aware that Christians, as intercessors, can pray for others and expect God to answer.

The *third* priority in a Christian's life should be church activities, social groups, work and all the hobbies that he might have.

Every Christian needs to assess whether he really allows God to have first place in his life. An assessment of this can be made by keeping a 24-hour calendar for about one week. Write down, on an hourly basis, each activity of each day. Observe how much time you give to God, how much time to your family, how much time to work and how much time to pleasure.

I don't mean to imply that God expects us to set aside eight hours each day for Him. But how much time do you give to God? Is it five, 10 minutes a day, or even less than that? How much time is devoted to television or newspapers that might be given to God? When you find a balance in your life, God will make the time spent more profitable. I believe that the majority of Christians could, if they planned their schedules properly, trim their average day back substantially and accomplish the same amount of work or perhaps more. But seek a balance. If business involvement requires that you sacrifice God's work or your family, it is *not* according to His plan.

8. *Avoid Indulgence.*

Every Christian, to achieve financial freedom, must avoid the indulgences of life.

The range in which God's will can be found is between Luke 9:23 when Christ said, "If anyone wishes to come after Me, let him deny himself, and take up his cross daily, and follow Me," and John 6:27, "Do not work for the food which perishes, but for the food which endures to eternal life, which the Son of Man shall give to you, for on Him the Father, even God, has set His seal."

Does your lifestyle fit within this range? Are you willing to trust God and deny yourself some indulgences? As you do, He will supply you even more. Unfortunately, most of us are self-indulgers, rarely passing up a want or desire, much less a need. But, in light of the needs around us, it is important that Christians assess their standards of living. Most of us can reduce our expenditures substantially without a real reduction in living standard.

9. *Christian Counseling.*

It is important to seek *good* Christian counseling whenever in doubt. "Without consultation, plans are frustrated, but with many counselors they succeed" (Proverbs 15:22). God admonishes us to seek counsel and not to rely solely on our own resources. In financial planning, many Christians become frustrated because they lack the necessary knowledge and then give up. God has supplied others with the ability to help in the area of finances. Seek them out.

A. The very first counselor to be used is the *spouse*. Many times God will provide the answer right within your own home. Husbands should not avoid their wives' counsel in the area of finance, for many times I have found the wife's suggestions to be useful and enlightened. Husbands and wives can frequently work out financial problems that would frustrate either of them separately.

Don't avoid the counsel of your own children, either. Let them know what your problems are, keep them involved. Allow them to know and understand why you must adjust your standard of living. Inform them that skating, boating, or movies may not fit into the new budget, and help them adjust to the necessary changes. Don't simply dictate to them, begin to communicate with them.

B. Let your need for counsel be made known to other Christians. Too many times we as Christians set up the facade that we have no problems. How can others help unless they are aware? Sometimes we act like hypocrites—we don't mind helping others, but we don't want to ask for help. We don't mind counseling someone who has a problem, but we don't want others to know when we have problems. It is not necesary to broadcast every problem throughout the Christian community, but at least allow others the opportunity to exercise their ministry.

C. If necessary, seek professional financial counseling. I would advise counseling *only* from a Christian source. Often good, sound financial counseling can come from a non-Christian source, but many of the things that you want to accomplish will be nonsense to the non-Christian.

So we can see, as we examine the concept of financial freedom, that God clearly outlines *when* a Christian is in financial bondage, as well as the steps that lead out. Begin to put these principles into practice in your life and share them with other Christians.

CHAPTER NINE

HOW TO PLAN A FINANCIAL PROGRAM

Planning is an essential element for any financial program, but it is particularly important for Christians. Too often Christians engage in arguments about whether or not they should do *any planning* at all. Those who argue no planning is necessary misunderstand what God said in Scripture about this area of finances. They argue that God does not *expect* us to do any planning but to rely on Him for everything. On the other side are Christians who say we should plan every second of our lives. Accordingly, they create plans so inflexible that they are no longer responsive to God's leading. This prospective is not correct either; somewhere in between lies the answer.

God is an orderly provider and expects us to be exactly the same. The physical world that we live in is not chaotic at all but is orderly and well planned. The universe stays in its path because God ordered it so. Atoms stay together because God so ordered them.

Finances are just another aspect of the Christian's life that God wants to manage. If we are stewards and God is indeed the owner, then it is *His* wisdom that we must seek. Therefore, it is necessary to go to God's Word for our plans.

HOW TO PLAN A FINANCIAL PROGRAM

Changed Attitude

The first part of the plan is to develop a changed attitude. Attitudes are not easily changed, just as habits are not easily changed. Part of an attitude change means you must do more than just make an initial *attempt* at creating a plan. You must first generate a plan according to God's conviction and then *utilize* it—apply God's principles in your everyday life.

If you make plans that are inflexible, they will only frustrate you and hinder God's work because you won't be able to live with them. In other words, develop plans that guide your financial life but also provide for some recreation and personal enjoyment as well.

Flexibility

Do not make plans that are totally dependent on financial increases. God's wisdom can be manifest through a reduction, if necessary, to redirect our lives. Naturally, we would all be happy to only get involved in ventures that result in profits. But sometimes God's will is accomplished by a loss rather than a gain.

Paul says in Philippians 4:12,13, "I know how to get along with humble means, and I also know how to live in prosperity; in any and every circumstance I have learned the secret of being filled and going hungry, both of having abundance and suffering need. I can do all things through Him who strengthens me." We should have that same perspective in planning. Learn to abase or abound. God will supply the strength to do all things for those in His will.

Guidelines

1. A Christian should learn to practice *patience* and moderation in each and every financial decision.

2. Implement a *positive* decision attitude.

3. Never get involved in financial decisions that require instant action, but allow God to take His course. The difference between a profit and a loss may well be the attitude with which we approach financial investments.

4. Avoid any *"get rich quick"* schemes, no matter how tempting they may seem to you.

5. Stick by your plans as long as you have peace about them; they're the plans for your life.

6. Do *not* be inflexible, but don't be vacillating, changing your plans just because somebody tells you something different.

Few people ever do *any* planning. But planning is an important aspect of our lives. The majority of businesses fail because they are undermanaged or undercapitalized, meaning that they have inadequate planning. It is futile to operate a business without a cash flow plan (income versus expenses) to allocate resources for paying bills. How could anyone maintain a business without knowing where the capital was coming from?

God has exactly the same plan in mind for a Christian's home, unfortunately most of us ignore it. How can anyone manage a home without coordinating income and expenses? As I mentioned earlier, we all have the knack of adjusting expenses to exceed income.

Very important attitudes are necessary to develop a sound, basic financial plan for the family. That plan falls into two areas—short-range goals and long-range goals.

Short-range Plans and Goals

Short-range plans are those which are happening *today*, and they require our attention today. Short-range plans are basically day-by-day occurrences.

For example, a housewife must have a short-range plan

for buying groceries. This will include how much she buys, how often she buys, the type of groceries that are necessary, etc. If she does no planning at all, before every meal she has to rush down to the store to buy more groceries. By the same token, there must be some plan for paying bills. Otherwise, when the paycheck comes, it seems like a windfall. The natural reaction is to spend all the money and ignore the bills that are not due immediately. Later there is no money to meet the obligations. Obviously, that is not an adequate plan.

In business, short-range plans include such things as what raw materials need to be ordered to manufacture the products for sale. If a business did no planning at all, every day the assembly line would have to shut down while they rushed out to purchase necessary materials. Obviously that is not practical so businesses make *goals* and develop plans to accomplish them.

Who Needs Goals?

Thus, as we have observed, *everyone* has short-range plans or goals. Some are carefully considered, others are more haphazard. If your short-range goal is to make money, you should review it because it is *not* a Christian objective. Having money as a goal means that you are really depending on yourself and not on God. As we discovered earlier, the mere ability to make money does not enrich you spiritually (Proverbs 2:4,5). But to do something that God has directed you to do will enrich you both spiritually and financially. Every Christian who has ever had money as a goal can testify that it does not satisfy. What are short-range goals from God's perspective? How can we develop plans to accomplish them?

HOW TO PLAN A FINANCIAL PROGRAM

Written Plans

A written plan provides a visible and objective standard to work toward. It is all right to have a mental goal as well, but unless you write it down, you will never be able to measure your progress. A written plan allows you to refer back to the original objective and keep on the track. It is also important to periodically update it to reflect new insights.

An example of a written plan inside the family is the budget. A budget has many functions. It will show where you are financially, how much you are presently spending, and how much you can spend according to your present income.

Very few if any families with financial difficulties have a written plan. Consequently, their financial lives stay in chaos. They have little idea of how much they owe or where the money goes each month. Predictably, at the end of a month the reaction is, "I don't know where all the money goes; I know it doesn't cost us that much to live." That's why a written plan is so essential for the family.

Short Range Goals

1. *Excellence.*

God wants us, as Christians, to *excel* at whatever we do to the very best of our ability. Too often Christians rationalize that it is somehow in God's plan to be second best. Thus they always hang back never really achieving their potential for fear that others will think them egotistical.

A Christian *can* excel at whatever he does without any egotism at all. Paul excelled and he had no egotism associated with it; Simon Peter excelled, though he remained a humble man. Each knew where his source of power was, each knew what God had asked him to do, and each would accept nothing less than excellence. We also should expect excellence as part of our short-range goals.

I Peter 4:11 says, "Whoever speaks, let him speak, as if it were, the utterances of God; whoever serves, let him do so as by the strength that God supplies; so that in all things God may be glorified through Jesus Christ . . . ." We are to use our abilities to God's glory.

It is equally important that wives and mothers excel at what they do. Usually it is the mother who becomes the "habit" teacher in the home; her attitudes are generally reflected by her children. If she excels at what she does and keeps the home well organized, she can be a great asset to home financial planning.

2. Limit Credit.

As previously mentioned, a part of short-range planning should be to limit or curtail the use of credit. This is a vitally important element of short-range plans. If you are looking for the very best plan that God has, adopt a cash-only basis as much as possible.

Often Christians say, "It isn't possible in our society today; we must have credit cards." That is absolutely *not* true. Many Christian families I know personally live on a non-credit basis and have done so for several years (with the exception of a home mortgage usually). Admittedly, it does take more planning, and it is necessary to establish check cashing privileges at most stores, but it *can* be done. The result will be a great sense of freedom and relief when there are no debts.

This does not mean that a Christian *cannot* use credit cards. So long as the accounts are current there is no violation of scriptural principles, but many Christians abuse the privilege of credit and *must* relinquish the use of credit cards. Most others *should* do so to avoid overspending.

3. Set Your Own Goals.

Establish your goals in relation to what God asks *you* to do, not what your neighbor asks you to do. As this principle is stated in a maxim, if you won't allow your neighbor to take out your appendix, don't allow him to invest your money! How does he know what plan God has in mind for you?

It is easy to get caught up in the frenzy of someone else's schemes. We see others apparently doing well and get talked into joining many half-baked ideas. The usual result is a loss of friendship, a loss of temper and a loss of money. So, if you allow somebody else to establish your short-range goals, then it is *you* who is going to suffer.

Unfortunately a great many people who really like what they do as a profession or a business feel frustrated because somebody else happens to be making more money in some speculative venture. Consequently they get involved in a program they know little or nothing about. The usual result is a costly financial education. There are limitless ways to lose money; one of the very best is through bad advice coupled with a little envy.

"As a result, we are no longer to be children, tossed here and there by waves, and carried about by every wind of doctrine, by the trickery of men, by craftiness in deceitful scheming " (Ephesians 4:14).

4. Work to Honor God.

Every Christian should stop and assess the following:
- Does my business always exemplify the Christian life?
- Will every one of my acts, day after day, be a witness to Christ?
- Can I do my work and be honoring to God?
- Does the company that I work for deal ethically with others?
- Am I helping others to violate some of the principles that I believe?
- Am I really providing a service or simply satisfying my own ambitions?

These are questions that every Christian *must* deal with if his work is to honor God. For instance, I believe the insurance trade can be a great service for families. But so often it is promoted on the basis of profit for the salesman rather than the needs of the client. Frequently individuals are sold too little insurance at too high a price, or too much insurance altogether. Few salesmen provide the *quality* and *quantity* of insurance that fits the exact needs of the buyer. Certainly it takes longer and means more effort, but in the end, not only will the salesman prosper, but the buyer will be a representative who will refer many more people to him.

Galatians 6:9, "And let us not lose heart in doing good, for in due time we shall reap if we do not grow weary." God's plan will not be widely accepted in the world. But just because the world doesn't agree does not mean that it is not perfect, because it is.

5. Establish a Sharing Plan.

One of the first goals a Christian family should establish is to tithe the first part of their income. This step is sometimes the most difficult, but it is also the most rewarding. Why? Because it is a material testimony to a spiritual commitment.

Long-range Planning

In *addition* to short-range planning, a Christian needs to assess his long-range goals. Any financial plan for Christians should be in harmony with prayer-guided long-range goals.

- — What are you here to achieve?
- — How are you going to accomplish God's plan?
- — If God blesses you with an abundance of money, what will you do with it?
- — What kind of a plan do you have for such an eventuality?

Too many Christians go through their entire lives without establishing any prayerful goals for the use of their wealth.

HOW TO PLAN A FINANCIAL PROGRAM

Many get trapped into a dogmatic, day-by-day routine. They have minimal short-range goals and almost no long-range goals at all. Understandably, many find themselves at the end of a 40- or 50-year period of work with an accumulation of wealth and in a quandary about where it should go. Others find themselves surrounded with problems and financial difficulties without any prearranged plan of action. Christians should look ahead and visualize what their long-range financial objectives are.

Not every Christian in our society will be wealthy, nor should everyone be wealthy. But everyone, wealthy or otherwise, has a responsibility to plan well, to have good, sound objectives, and to operate according to God's principles. The *truly* successful Christians in this world are those who have thoroughly acknowledged God's ownership, have accepted their stewardship and have made their plans accordingly.

A Christian should establish long-range goals *only after* much personal and family prayer. The following biblical principles should be the cornerstone of all such goals.

Accept the Necessity to Plan

The first requirement is to recognize the *need* to do long-range planning. Just as in your short-range plans, your long-range plans should be written. Often, by the very act of writing down what you hope to accomplish, God will provide an insight into His plan.

Your long-range goals should reflect your personal financial objectives, a plan for the surplus and an after-death plan. As previously discussed, everything in the Lord's will is an orderly, progressive plan. God promises to supply His wisdom to all who seek it. "For by Me your days will be multiplied, and years of life will be added to you" (Proverbs 9:11). God is saying that by observing *His* ways you can add additional years to your life.

He also says: "For which one of you, when he wants to build a tower, does not first sit down and calculate the cost, to see if he has enough to complete it? Otherwise, when he has laid a foundation, and is not able to finish, all who observe it begin to ridicule him, saying, 'This man began to build and was not able to finish' " (Luke 14:28-30).

Long-range Goals

1. Set a Maximum Goal.

A Christian should have a goal of how much he wants to accumulate — *maximum, not minimum.* You need to think in terms of storing for provision rather than storing for protection.

Christians who have minimum financial objectives have not really assessed what's happening to this economy. It is possible that God has asked some Christians to store up for the future needs of others, but the issue again relates to attitude. Is your attitude one of hoarding or sharing?

When God sent Joseph to Egypt, did he hoard the food that he put aside or did he store it for the time when it would be needed? Those who are not sharing in good times certainly will not do so in difficult times.

Once a maximum goal is established, peer approval will cease to be important, and the truth of Proverbs 11:28 will be more apparent in the Christian's life: "He who trusts in his riches will fall, but the righteous will flourish like the green leaf." Those who fail to acknowledge this in our society have already been identified by the Lord. Ezekiel 7:19 states: "They shall fling their silver into the streets, and their gold shall become an abhorrent thing; their silver and their gold shall not be able to deliver them in the day of the wrath of the Lord. They cannot satisfy their appetite, nor can they fill their stomachs, for their iniquity has become an occasion of stumbling."

2. *Surplus Plan.*

You should have a long-range plan for what to do with the surplus God supplies. How much should you return to the Lord's work? How much should you supply to your family? How much should you invest? Should you provide everything your children ask for? (Many times, as a rationalization for an overcommitment to work, or out of guilt, we will purchase *things* for our children instead of spending time with them.)

Each Christian must assess for himself God's plan for the surplus. However, God does provide some clear guidelines for doing this.

In I Corinthians 3:12,13 it states, "Now if any man builds upon the foundation with gold, silver, precious stones, wood, hay, straw, each man's work will become evident; for the day will show it, because it is to be revealed with fire; and the fire itself will test the quality of each man's work." What is this work that God refers to? Revelation 2:19, has the answer, "I know your deeds, and your love and faith and service and perseverance, and that your deeds of late are greater than at first." Will God be able to say to you when He returns, "Well done, My good and faithful servant"?

Establish a surplus plan while the opportunity and the capability exists. *Do not* count on future events to support God's work. In other words, if you have money stored and God lays a need on you, give right then. It may even be necessary to disregard some tax advantages. Many people retain investments to take maximum advantage of the tax law. I don't disagree with the "logic" of that; I'd rather have God as my partner in a venture than the government.

God does not give us the ability to generate money so that we can hoard it because it then works against us. The Lord is quite capable of investing His money as He sees the need. It is our responsibility and privilege as stewards to be used as funnels for the funds used in His work. If we refuse, God will simply pass us by and find someone who will.

3. Obey God's Principles.

In formulating your long-range plans, pay specific attention to God's principles:

Honesty. Never allow yourself to be trapped into anything that is unethical, immoral or dishonest, no matter how inviting it seems. Proverbs 16:8 says, "Better is a little with righteousness than great income with injustice." So it is important that we observe honesty in all of our plans. There aren't any small lies, there are just lies. There aren't any small thefts, there are just thefts.

Employee Welfare. Christian employers have an absolute responsibility to *care* for their employees. A part of your long-range planning in your business involves the welfare of your employees. If you expect a fair day's work, pay a fair day's wage.

A part of company profits belongs not only to management, but also to the employees. God has a personal management plan in Scripture that will revolutionize a business. But too often Christian employers are more intent on making money than providing for the welfare of employees. I Timothy 5:18 says, "For the Scripture says, 'You shall not muzzle the ox while he is threshing' and 'The laborer is worthy of his wages.' " Christian employers should be aware that not only do they have additional authority, but additional responsibility as well.

Concern for Others. Often opportunities will arise to take unfair advantage of others. You must precondition your attitude to avoid any temptation. "Do not rob the poor because he is poor, or crush the afflicted at the gate; for the Lord will plead their case, and take the life of those who rob them" (Proverbs 22:22,23).

Obey the Law. God demands obedience to the law in your long-range plans. I speak here specifically of tax laws. There are two terms used to describe tax planning. One is *tax avoidance*, taking all the legal remedies available under the law, while another is *tax evasion*, taking all the legal remedies plus some not allowed within the boundaries of the law. The lines between the two are very, very narrow and are easily crossed.

In counseling, I find many Christians violate the tax laws and rationalize it. People who would not think of robbing a bank feel justified in stealing from the government. I object to the highly lopsided tax structure of our system as much as anybody, but to illegally avoid the debt due is stealing. It is easy to rationalize because the government is a large, inflexible institution, but it is still stealing.

Proverbs 15:27 states, "He who profits illicitly troubles his own house, but he who hates bribes will live." Take maximum advantage of every tax law in existence: charitable giving, tax sheltering, depreciation, expenses and any other step, but be careful not to cross the line and become involved in tax evasion and theft.

4. A Long-range Family Plan.

(A) A family living plan. Every Christian must establish a long-range family plan. What do you want for your family? Have you ever brought your family together to pray about *how* God wants you to live?

God cares about the house you live in, the car you drive, where you work, whether your wife should work, your children's college and even the food you eat. Have you ever prayed over these things? If you have not, how can you expect to determine exactly what God's will for your family is?

Can you ever store *enough* to protect your family? I don't believe so. The best you can do is short-term provision. God has a better plan for every Christian that seeks His wisdom. When God says, "Be not anxious," that does *not* mean to be unconcerned or imprudent. There is a distinct difference between concern or preparedness and worry. Later we will discuss how you can plan for your family using God's principles.

(B) Establish priorities. Your long-range goals should focus on financial priorities. Remember, how we defined

the priorities of needs, wants and desires? Needs are basic living requirements, wants are to improve our standard of living and desires are the luxuries of affluence.

Establish these priorities with your family. Help them to understand the difference between a need, a want and a desire, particularly children. When your child approaches you with a request, sit down with him and discuss whether it is a need, a want or a desire.

If it is a need, it should be supplied. This includes medical attention, dental work, food, clothing or shelter— all within limits.

But if it is a want or a desire, you should be able to establish the fact that if he wants it, assuming you agree, perhaps he should earn it. When a child learns that he must earn some of his wants and desires, a quick adjustment is made. A movie is weighed against a new baseball bat, or a nonsense toy against a coin for his collection.

The important factor here is *you!* Be consistent and fair but firm. Just as God will not grant us whims that work to our detriment, so you must hold the same position with your children.

Be a walking, talking testimony to your children, your Christian friends and your non-Christian friends. I don't mean that you have to shout from the rooftops—*you do not*! But if you live the Christian life, adjusting to a disciplined style of living, you will be a testimony throughout your entire community.

In Luke 16:14 we are told, "Now the Pharisees, who were lovers of money, were listening to all these things, and they were scoffing at Him." Will you allow the scoffers to establish your plans and goals by default? If not, you must act positively.

(C) Have a family sharing plan. Why should God trust you with a surplus? Does your family manage money well? Do your children understand the proper attitudes about material possessions? What plans do the other members of your family have for the money that they earn? Are they

willing to tithe openly and willingly without you pressuring them? A part of every Christian's plan for sharing must include his family. Bring them into the decision and *pray* as a family.

(D) Have an estate plan. Do you have a plan for how much to leave to your family? In other words, an after-death plan? One based on provision not *protection*? I hope by now you realize you cannot *protect* your family. Those who store up great amounts of life insurance seeking after-death protection for their families are fooling themselves. We attempt to build great walled cities around our families because we believe it is necessary to protect them against everything. But there is a better way. God's plan will revolutionize our concept of protection in the last days. It will be as a "body" that we exist both during life and after. In a later section we will examine the practical *amount* for an estate or inheritance plan.

(E) Have a contingency plan. It is important to state that a Christian must establish a contingency plan in the event that he accumulates wealth faster than anticipated. Scripture is clear on this point; God's surplus is to be shared. In Proverbs 11:24,25 we find, "There is one who scatters, yet increases all the more, and there is one who withholds what is justly due, but it results only in want. The generous man will be prosperous, and he who waters will himself be watered." *This* is God's plan for Christians, but unless one has a predetermined plan for these increases, expenses will be adjusted to offset any additional increases. Consequently, there will never be a surplus to share.

CHAPTER TEN

WHY ACCUMULATE WEALTH?

Earlier we reviewed the biblical definition of wealth, recognizing that it related not to just our money, but our homes, our families, our abilities, our intelligence, our educations—*everything* that we have. We also discovered that God's perspective of our wealth is always *centered around our* attitudes.

Keeping that in mind, why is it that people accumulate wealth? Accumulation means more than just storing away; it also refers to making, using, spending and sharing wealth.

As discussed previously, money can be used for the comfort and convenience of our families. It can be used to provide the needs of others. It can be used to spread the gospel. Or it can be used for destructive purposes (such as buying bombs or guns).

Attitude will determine its uses, so it is vital for us to discover what attitudes God wants us to have. Why does He allow us to accumulate wealth? What are the limits of our accumulation? Can we define what God's will is so that we can have the peace that He promises?

Money, if it is misused, as in the case of the rich young ruler (Matthew 19:16-30), can be an object of devotion and idolatry. Love of money has separated families and shattered friendships. Countless marriages have split up over the love of, or the misuse of, money. Christians, therefore, must assess *why* they accumulate money in the light of God's principles.

Ministry of Money?

Many Christians have the ability to accumulate large amounts of wealth. Virtually everyone in America has the potential of accumulating a surplus. What we consider to be a *minimum* standard of living is significantly above that experienced in most other parts of the world. It is not unheard of in our society for someone living on a small fixed income to accumulate tens of thousands of dollars through scrimping and sacrificing. With this potential, it becomes vital that God's attitude about accumulating money become a part of our personalities.

God will provide a ministry in money for Christians attuned to His plan. But it is a ministry of sharing, not of selfishness. A Christian who reclaims ownership of his finances steps right out of God's will. Others, who share as God asks, receive the blessings of the Lord and the great harvest promised in Scripture. Once a Christian accepts money as a *ministry,* a whole new area of God's will opens up.

In II Corinthians 9:8, we are told, "And God is able to make all grace abound to you, that always having all sufficiency in everything, you may have an abundance for every good deed." What are the absolute promises given here?

1. God will make all *grace* abound in each one of us.
2. We will always have *sufficiency* for our needs.
3. We will have an *abundance* for other good deeds.

If you have the ability to make money, as a Christian, you *must* have the desire to share. If you are making money and not sharing it, you can be absolutely certain that you are *not* within God's will and probably that money is being supplied from another source.

It's important to realize, too, that some more old religious folklore comes to the fore in this area: to give money is gracious, but to make it is a sin. *Wrong!* God said giving is a gift, and, as we discussed earlier, if giving money is a gift from God, making it must also be a gift from Him. Christians should accept the principle that there is nothing wrong with making money, provided you do so *within* God's plan.

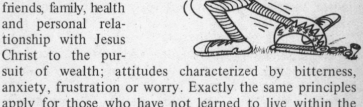

Do not violate the principles that God established. Remember the symptoms: sacrifice of friends, family, health and personal relationship with Jesus Christ to the pursuit of wealth; attitudes characterized by bitterness, anxiety, frustration or worry. Exactly the same principles apply for those who have not learned to live within the provision that God has supplied.

Why Do People Accumulate Wealth?

As you read this section, keep in mind the *range* of God's will in Scripture. By understanding the limits of God's plan you can evaluate your own position.

1. Others Advise It.

Many people get into investments, businesses or other ventures simply because someone else advises them to do so. They don't have any clear personal plans or goals. Most have *no plans* either short-range or long-range. If God supplied them an abundance, they would not really have a plan for sharing, re-investing or saving. They simply

commit their resources to some program because somebody else thinks it is a good idea. Usually they have little
or no knowledge about the use of their money and react
to investment fluctuations with anxiety or alarm. What
is the proper attitude?

In Proverbs 15:22, God states, "Without consultation,
plans are frustrated, but with many counselors they
succeed." Proverbs 18:15 says, "The mind of the prudent
acquires knowledge . . . ." Paraphrased this says, "It is
the wise man who seeks many counselors." Christians
are advised by God to seek many counselors on everything because with too few counselors plans go astray.

But, in Ephesians 4:14 Paul expresses the other end
of the range: "As a result, we are no longer to be children,
tossed here and there by waves, and carried about by every
wind of doctrine, by the trickery of men, by craftiness in
deceitful scheming."

Therefore, according to God's plan, we are to seek
counsel, especially in the area of investments and management of money. But we must weigh everything against
His Word. *Listen* to new ideas around you, but seek
God's direction before any action is taken. Also, seek the
counsel of your spouse; many times God supplies the
necessary wisdom within your own home.

Make the following assessments for all advice. First,
is it within God's plan at all? Then, is it compatible with
your plans? Don't get involved in an investment simply
because somebody has a new idea. Do so only because
you believe it enhances your ministry and your family
life and you feel a clear sense of peace about it.

2. Envy of Others.

Many people accumulate money simply because they
envy other people. They fall into the trap of the "keeping
up with the Joneses" syndrome.

They could easily identify with a character by the name
of *Ernie Envy.* Now old Ernie is a "secret service Christian"
(meaning that nobody can tell from his activities if he is or

isn't a Christian). Ernie maintains a "follow-the-leader" attitude. He moved into a large home because his friend Bill got a new job. Then, because all of his neighbors had new cars, Ernie had to get one, too.

By this time Ernie recognized he was in deep water and sinking, but then a new challenge appeared. One of his closest friends was selling a new franchise product and really making a "killing." Ernie heard how easy it was. All you had to do was sell two or three of your friends the same idea and you could "get rich quick."

Ernie had never sold anything in his life, and this sounded a little fishy, but his basic envy and greed overcame any internal hesitation. So he borrowed the money to buy into the franchise.

Several months later Ernie lost most of his franchise fee and several friends when the whole scheme fell apart. Now, Ernie is ashamed to even talk about Christ because of his personal lifestyle. Ernie never has to worry about a face-to-face encounter with Satan because they're both headed in the same direction . . .

This plan clearly is not within God's will for a Christian. Therefore, there is no provision for this attitude in the Bible. "But as for me, my feet came close to stumbling; my steps had almost slipped. For I was envious of the arrogant, as I saw the prosperity of the wicked" (Psalms 73: 2,3). In other words, we are not to envy those who are storing up riches. Unfortunately, it is easy to fall into this trap. We begin to envy others and allow our lifestyles to be dictated by those around us.

Advertising promotes this attitude as acceptable, but God does not! "And He said to them, 'Beware and be on your guard against every form of greed; for not even when one has an abundance does his life consist of his possessions' " (Luke 12:15).

3. *Game of It.*

This is the plan that ensnares both Christians and non-Christians alike. Many people accumulate money as a game; they match themselves against others relentlessly. The world system heavily promotes this concept. We elevate the *winners* regardless of how they played the *game*. The only problem is that the game quickly overwhelms the players. Participants get so wrapped up in the contest that they sacrifice family, friends or health to keep winning.

Walter Winner portrays their lifestyle. Walter started his "gaming" career early in life. He was the kid in high school who knew *all* the rules. He also tested most of them to see how much he could get away with. Walter never could keep any real friends because,somehow, he always got involved in conflicts with them, particularly when they disagreed with him. Walter made it through college and into one of the professions, but his work quickly bored him since it was no fun competing against himself.

So Walter began to diversify into investments and business. And he did well, cutting every corner possible and using every friend available. Soon Walter was well known as an investor and a "wheeler-dealer." Although he wouldn't purposely cheat anyone, he seemed to always come out on the high side.

He gave to his church, but not in relation to what he received. He felt it was dumb to give more than you could write off in taxes. Besides, if he gave away the investments that were losers, he could get the same tax deduction. Oh, yes, Walter also failed to use any of his surplus, either for his family or for others. After all, almost all of the money was needed to expand his investment portfolio. . .

The purpose in a game is entertainment, and non-Christians entertain themselves in the area of money. God does not provide this alternative for the Christian. Those who get involved with the game of making money are soon overcome by their own pastime. They quickly lose sight of why they have money. They also lose sight of their families for they are so involved with the game that *everybody* becomes a pawn.

WHY ACCUMULATE WEALTH?

God's attitude in this area is described in Psalms 17:13, 14: "Arise, O Lord, confront him, bring him low; deliver my soul from the wicked with Thy sword, from men with Thy hand, O Lord, from men of the world, whose portion is in this life; and whose belly Thou dost fill with Thy treasure; they are satisfied with children, and leave their abundance to their babes."

As we discussed earlier, one of the best ways to avoid this trap is through a long-range plan for surplus. Commit a *large* portion of each investment to the Lord's work, today. You will know quickly whether that money is coming from God or Satan. If it is coming from Satan, I'll guarantee you that he will withdraw the supply because he will not continue to prosper someone who gives of the bounty to the Lord.

The results are predictable; there will be a change in your attitude and perhaps even in the supply. Then the supply will begin coming in from God if that is His plan for your life. By doing so, this will transfer your ability from serving self to serving God.

4. Self-esteem.

Those who accumulate money for self-esteem do so in order that others might look upon them with envy. This is a very worldly motive for accumulating money, and yet it characterizes many Christians.

Those who suffer under this motive use their money in an attempt to buy esteem even from their own families. They want people to cater to them, to elevate them and to always yield to their way. These people never share with anyone except to *promote themselves.* They do nothing anonymously; when they give they give in sight of other people. And they expect esteem back for it.

Our characters for this attitude are *Sam Superior* and his wife *Sally Society.* Sam tries to convince everyone that he came up the hard way. He points out that he never had a new sports car in high school. He worked his way through college on the polo team and then started at the "bottom" in business as a junior vice-president in his father's factory.

Sam and Sally go to church every Sunday (except for an occasional Sunday golf game) where Sam is the chief elder. They have several pews named after them and never fail to pledge to the building program. Neither are sure exactly how to become a Christian but assume it must be by osmosis. Their names are always appearing in the society pages in connection with charitable benefits.

Sam thinks life has been pretty good to him, except he can't understand why his daughter ran away and his youngest son dropped out of school to live with some "hippies."

He's sure Sally was right in telling him to get rid of that young preacher who talked about knowing God personally. And he agrees with her that the church has enough problems without inviting a bunch of strangers to visit like that preacher keeps suggesting . . .

What is the range? None. A Christian cannot accumulate for self-esteem within God's plan. We can find many references in Scripture that deal with this attitude, one of them being I Timothy 6:17: "Instruct those who are rich in this present world not to be conceited or to fix their hope on the uncertainty of riches, but on God, who richly supplies us with all things to enjoy."

Esteem and importance will fade as quickly as the money. Are you working for the esteem of men or the rewards of God?

5. *The Love of Money.*

Those who *love* money wouldn't part with it for anything—not even for esteem. Their lives are characterized by hoarding and abasement. They may have accumulated thousands, tens of thousands or even millions, but the loss of even a few dollars is traumatic. They become embittered, nervous, frustrated and angry when others invade their financial domain. This is a form of idol worship, just as surely as worshipping pagan images of clay or metal.

WHY ACCUMULATE WEALTH?

Our character for this example will be *Greg Greed*. Greg has practiced the worldly art of hoarding for many years now. It is difficult to say exactly when it all began, but probably even in his childhood. Everybody knows and dislikes Greg, and many fear him. It is said that Greg would cheat his own brother if there were a profit in it.

Unfortunately, Greg doesn't see himself that way. He believes these are all shrewd business deals. After all, everybody has to look out for themselves. Greg's life is characterized by one big emotional roller coaster. If his business and investments are doing well, he feels good and is happy around the home and office. But, if his investments drop, even a little bit, he is mean, irritable and even hostile.

Greg's total downfall is due when a real economic reversal occurs. Then he will be a statistic in the paper, either a mental breakdown or a suicide...

Unfortunately, this attitude prevails in many Christians; they cling to every material possession they can get their hands on. Someone who is trapped by the love of money would let his family do without rather than part with his most precious possession. Once again we are reminded in I Timothy 6:10, "For the love of money is a root of all sorts of evil, and some by longing for it have wandered away from the faith, and pierced themselves with many a pang." In Hebrews 13:5 we are told, "Let your way of life be free from the love of money, being content with what you have; for He Himself has said, 'I will never desert you, nor will I ever forsake you.'"

The love of money separates us from God. What foolishness it is for a Christian to fall into this trap. "For what is a man profited if he gains the whole world, and loses or forfeits himself?" (Luke 9:25).

If I could describe the general attitude of someone who loves money, I would say it is an inability to ever accept a loss or to share—except for profit.

I have known many Christians who suffered from the love of money in one degree or another. In many instances, God convicted them that the only way they would ever really know peace in their lives was to trust Him *totally*. Generally, for them to trust Him required separation from their abundance of money.

Those captured by their money must cease storing and hoarding and begin sharing with others. If they don't do this voluntarily, one day they will be comparing ash heaps with others who failed to follow God's plan.

6. *Protection.*

People accumulate money for protection. On the surface this sounds proper; certainly we need to protect ourselves, don't we?

Obviously, if we don't know what is going to happen in the future, we should protect against future events. This kind of logic causes Christians to accumulate large amounts of money for *protection*. But, if we look below the surface, it is apparent that they don't really trust God enough to *believe* that He can supply their needs. So they begin to stash it away.

Those pursuing protection don't really love money, nor are they accumulating money for esteem. They are just nervous and anxious over what *might* happen in the future.

At first, the goal is a few hundred dollars, just to tide them over, in case. Then, the attitude adjusts quickly and that few hundred becomes a few thousand. Allowed to continue unabated, this same attitude will grow forever and will never be enough.

This attitude is also displayed through storing large hoards of life insurance, disability insurance, liability insurance or massive amounts of assets. Understand, none of these are bad in themselves; it is only through misuse that they become corruptive.

Willie Worrier is our example of this attitude. Willie began his retirement savings program the first week he started working. By the time he met the right girl and settled down, he had a tidy nest egg. But he couldn't use any of it, after all, he had bigger responsibilities then.

Willie had a good job with an above average income, but he never could get far enough "ahead" to share much. He believed in God all right, but he didn't believe in the tithe. After all, doesn't the Bible say someplace, "God helps those who help themselves?"

Willie carried plenty of insurance. He had disability, liability, casualty, health, life and insurance-policy insurance. After working most of his life, squirreling every extra penny away, Willie was approaching his life long ambition — *retirement.* Then, through a castastrophe almost all the funds Willie had were lost, gone in almost no time. Willie became nearly neurotic, crying and bemoaning the fact that *God* had let this happen to him. . .

Willie could be any Christian in our generation, storing for that elusive "rainy day." Passing by the *only* investment program with a written guarantee — God's. I don't mean to say that Christians shouldn't save; they should! God may also convict some to "store," but He will do so only to committed Christians who have the correct attitudes about sharing.

Many Christians hoard resources because they fear the future and lack the ability to trust in God and to believe that He can supply their needs. Thus they attempt to protect themselves.

This obsession with protection takes away that which God would have us live by as Christians, faith and trust in Him. "Offer to God a sacrifice of thanksgiving, and pay your vows to the Most High; and call upon Me in the day of trouble; I shall rescue you, and you shall honor

Me" (Psalms 50:14,15).

Anxiety over the future traps many Christians into *protection*. Having stepped out of God's will, they are no longer trusting in Him but in worldly things. When these worldly things collapse around them, their faith collapses also. God says to *provide* for the family, but one who seeks protection is blind.

7. A Spiritual Gift.

As I looked through Scripture studying this aspect of Christian finances, it became very apparent that there is only *one* reason that God supplies a *surplus* of wealth to a Christian—so that he will have enough to provide for the needs of others. Because *true* wealth comes with the gift of giving. God promises His blessings to all who freely give and promises His curse on those who hoard, steal, covet or idolize.

Paul defines the reason for having wealth as meeting the needs of the saints. The gift of giving is defined as the foundation for a life of selfless devotion to others. "You will be enriched in everything for all liberality, which through us is producing thanksgiving to God" (II Corinthians 9:11).

Being a wealthy Christian establishes a responsibility greater than being a poor Christian. Being rich or being poor is a matter of providence in God's will, and He will give us only that which we are capable of handling. But the duties and responsibilities of wealth are very heavy because of the temptations. You can step outside of God's plan simply by *attitude*.

A wealthy Christian needs only to adjust his lifestyle to lavishness and indulgence to totally buffer God's direction. The poor Christian usually has a clear-cut decision of honesty versus dishonesty.

Proverbs 30:8b,9a, says, "Feed me with the food that is my portion, lest I be full and deny Thee and say, 'Who is the Lord?' " So we see that becoming content without God in our abundance is a much more subtle sin than stealing. We just slip outside of God's will and never realize it until calamity hits.

The responsibility of Christians is awesome and sobering. God, in His eternal plan, has decided to use *us* to supply His work. One day, we must all stand before God and give an account of what we have done on this earth with *His* resources. If a Christian accepts God's plan for his life and resources, he will store up treasures in heaven that will last an eternity.

Why does God provide an accumulation of wealth? So His people can exercise *the spiritual gift of giving.*

CHAPTER ELEVEN

HOW MUCH IS ENOUGH?

Now that we've studied aspects of *why* Christians are to accumulate wealth, let's examine God's Word to determine the range we are to observe. How can you tell when your finances are in balance? When are you accumulating too much? Can you tell when you have stepped outside the range of provision and begun to protect rather than provide? How much should you leave to your children? How much should you invest or hold for retirement?

1. Current Provision.

Every Christian should be concerned with providing for his family. But how much is enough? Of course, there is no magic formula that can be uniformly applied to every family. There are several variables that need to be considered such as the ages of the family members, the size of the family, educational needs, personal aspirations and where the family lives.

But other factors should be taken into consideration in making any decisions about future provision:

    a. God's plan for your life.

    b. Present spending level.

    c. Future income potential.

    d. Dependability of present income.

    e. Potential vocational changes.

As you can see, there are many individual factors to

be considered. However, there are certain basic decisions that can be made:

    a. Each Christian should adjust his lifestyle until it fits the plan that God has for *his* life.

    b. A minimum savings plan for purchases should be started.

    c. A minimum expense buffer should be established.

    d. Future education plans should be made.

Just as protection is wrong, so is too little provision or none at all. Neglect occurs when we have the capability of supplying our family's needs but fail to do so.

If the circumstances change so that we are no longer able to live within a reasonable budget, God will provide for our needs beyond any doubt. But, we have the requirement from God to be prudent.

What are the requirements for us as Christians to provide for our families? Let's look at a parable in Proverbs 6:6-11. "Go to the ant, O sluggard, observe her ways and be wise, which, having no chief, officer or ruler, prepares her food in the summer, and gathers her provision in the harvest. How long will you lie down, O sluggard? When will you arise from your sleep? 'A little sleep, a little slumber, a little folding of the hands to rest' — and your poverty will come in like a vagabond, and your need like an armed man."

God uses this parable to tell us that if we are slack and do not earn our way, poverty will come upon us and our families. This same admonition to work is found in I Timothy 5:8. We *must* provide for our families, lest we be considered less than an infidel. But ants *never* hoard; they store only that which they can eventually use.

The other end of the range is expressed by these verses: "For all these things the nations of the world eagerly seek; but your Father knows that you need these things. But seek for His Kingdom, and these things shall be added to you" (Luke 12:30,31). Do you recognize the importance of this principle? While God expects us to provide for our families and allows no folding of hands, no attitudes of laziness, He also supplies each and every one of our needs. And He will *never* allow us to lack for anything when we follow His principles.

2. Investment Reserves.

How much is enough for investment reserves? Obviously, if a part of God's plan for your life is to invest money, you must determine just how much that should be. But how do you know when you have gone beyond investment reserves into that area of hoarding?

As noted so many times in the past, it all revolves around your *attitude.* First, ask yourself these questions: Why am I investing? What kind of a plan for the surplus do I have?

As an investor, you must retain some funds out of each investment to make additional investments. But, too often, Christians believe that setting aside these funds comes first, and they take the bulk of the proceeds from one investment and put it into another one. This is an easily rationalized action, usually with an eye on the tax advantages and sometimes with the plan of multiplying God's portion.

Neither case is scriptural, however. God is capable of using His money in His ministry *today.* After every economic downturn there are many disappointed Christian investors. They kept the Lord's money for years, planning to give it to Him, but never taking the opportunity to share in His work. Then one day it is all gone, consumed as chaff and fodder.

Few Christians have the proper perspective on investments. On one side stand those who believe Christians should not be involved at all. On the other side stand those who are indistinguishable from the world.

HOW MUCH IS ENOUGH?

I believe one aspect of God's will in this area is found in the previously discussed parable of the stewards in Luke 19:12-24. Let's review this parable from another viewpoint in relation to making investments. Beginning in verse 20 where the nobleman confronts the third servant: "'And the other came, saying, "Master, behold your mina, which I kept put away in a handkerchief; for I was afraid of you, because you are an exacting man; you take up what you did not lay down, and reap what you did not sow." He said to him, "By your own words I will judge you, you worthless slave. Did you know that I am an exacting man, taking up what I did not lay down, and reaping what I did not sow? Then why did you not put the money in the bank, and having come, I would have collected it with interest?" And he said to the bystanders, "Take the mina away from him, and give it to the one who has the ten minas."'"

We can learn many things from this parable of the talents:

a. God is the *owner*, and He only gives us what He wishes us to handle.
b. He gives to each according to his *ability*.
c. As we prove to be more trustworthy, He entrusts much more to us.
d. He takes from those who are untrustworthy and gives to the faithful.
e. God expects multiplication, not just maintenance. It is a worthless servant who tries to withhold the bounty of his efforts.

In fact, God gives the *requirement* to invest. (So God has nothing against investments in a Christian's life at all.) But also, understand the servants' attitudes. They knew they weren't the *owners.* Even the worthless one recognized this, and he returned to the nobleman what was his. Two recognized their duty to use their abilities, the third refused. Thus, if God gives us the requirement to invest and multiply, He will supply only what we are capable of handling. As we show our faithfulness, He will give us even more. Our responsibility is to return it to His work.

I believe the other end of the range is expressed in II Corinthians 9:10,11. "Now He who supplies seed to the sower and bread for the food, will supply and multiply your seed for sowing and increase the harvest of your righteousness; you will be enriched in everything for all liberality, which through us is producing thanksgiving to God."

God is the perfect partner in any investment program. It is *He* who supplies all of the seed to be planted. We plant it, He multiplies it. What could be simpler? And so any investment program ought to be based around multiplying the assets that God supplies and returning the bulk of the crop. The seeds that we retain then bring in a greater harvest the next time.

Every Christian should remember, no matter how fertile the soil is, it remains barren without rain from God. Also, it is foolish to plow, till and fertilize the soil and never put in any seeds, for then you can anticipate a large crop of tares and weeds.

3. Retirement-Savings.

Retirement provision is a subject about which many Christians are confused. As previously noted, we have developed a mania about retirement savings and the necessity for storing large amounts of assets. Many people think they need to retire and spend much more than they did during working years. That is just not true. Once you set a pattern for living during your life, it will not change substantially after retirement, except in most cases to go down. If a Christian has learned to adjust his standard of living during his income years, then retirement will be a comfortable adjustment. The Christian who accumulates hoards of money to be used for retirement is being deceived.

Who can best provide for your retirement years, God

or man? Begin to assess right now how much you will really need later. How many clothes can you buy and how many trips can you take? How much food can you eat? Reassess your *need* for retirement and take a portion of that which you don't consider *necessary* and give it to the Lord's ministry today. God will not let a Christian suffer who has the right attitude.

Where does a retirement (or savings) program fit in God's plan? "There is precious treasure and oil in the dwelling of the wise, but a foolish man swallows it up" (Proverbs 21:20). Thus God declares that we *should* save something for the future. This may include saving for purchases or, ultimately, retirement.

But it is important that Christians get their priorities straight. There is nothing wrong with retirement, but there is something wrong with hoarding, whatever its guise.

Our whole concept of retirement is nonsense. We have been conditioned to believe that people lose their usefulness when they get to be 60 or 65 years old. Such is not the case. Many of the apostles did their greatest work after the time we would have considered them to be "old men." When Paul admonished Timothy not to let anybody mock him because of his youth, Timothy was over 40 years old at the time. So at what point should we really retire? If a Christian has a good, full life and enjoys what he does, he will be useful throughout his entire life span — not just in his early years. No, there is nothing wrong with saving for retirement in moderation. But, yes, there is something wrong with storing unnecessarily, believing that is the *only* way to provide for later years.

The other end on the range of God's will in this area can be found in Luke 12:16-20. "And He told them a parable saying, 'The land of a certain rich man was very productive. And he began reasoning to himself, saying, "What shall I do, since I have no place to store my crops?" And he said, "This is what I will do: I will tear down my barns and build larger ones, and there I will store my grain and my goods. And I will say to my soul, 'Soul, you have many goods laid up for many years to come; take your ease, eat, drink and be merry.' " But God said to him, "You fool! This very night your soul is required of you; and now who will own what you prepared?" ' "

Can you see God's attitude through this parable? It says that the man was rich, but God did not condemn him for his wealth. His downfall came when he had an *increase* in his income. Knowing he didn't have enough room in his barns, what did he decide to do? *Hoard!* Build larger barns to store his crops and then . . . contentment without God. Rather than seeking God's plan for the surplus, he decided to store it away. That *is not* the plan that God has in mind for Christians.

So to summarize this area, lest I leave you with some misconception, there is nothing wrong with retirement planning. But there is something wrong with living for retirement. There is nothing wrong with saving either, except where *protection* against the world is the motive.

Reassess your attitudes as a Christian. Is there something different about your life from that of the non-Christian's? Are you really worried that if you don't store now you will have to do without later? Do you *believe* that God is capable of supplying in your old age or is your faith a myth?

4. Inheritance.

If I had to identify the area of Christian finances that is least understood, I would have to vote for inheritance. Not only do many people wreck their lives by hoarding, but they also wreck the lives of their children and children's children with an abundant inheritance. The result of giving large amounts of money to those who are untrained in the use of money can be seen in the parable of the prodigal son, Luke 15:11-24.

At least the father in this parable had enough sense to give his son the inheritance while he was living. He then had the opportunity to provide his son with counseling.

Even so, the result of the inheritance was trouble for the recipient.

Large amounts of money given to children will usually be squandered to their disservice, and large amounts of money stored up for children in trust can be used to buffer them from God's will. Is that your wish? Allow your children the joy of earning their own way. This doesn't mean´ to impoverish them; provide for your family, but *do not* buffer them with great hoards of money.

God's will concerning inheritances is partly expressed in Ecclesiastes 6:3. "If a man fathers a hundred children and lives many years, however many they be, but his soul is not satisfied with good things, and he does not even have a proper burial, then I say, 'Better a miscarriage than he.' " This parable denotes the necessity of leaving the family *some* provision. God said that as godly men we leave our children's children an inheritance, but that inheritance is *spiritual.*

The other aspect of God's will can be found in Psalms 37:25,26. "I have been young, and now I am old; yet I have not seen the righteous forsaken, or his descendants begging bread. All day long he is gracious and lends; and his descendants are a blessing."

It becomes very obvious that the same promises *God* makes about lifetime provision extend from generation to generation. *Provide* for your family within reason. Trust God for their protection. God promises He will not let your offspring be forsaken and go begging bread.

HOW MUCH IS ENOUGH?

Summary

I have listed below the pertinent points from God's Word dealing with *why people accumulate wealth* and *how much is enough.*

1. *Because others advise it.* A Christian should *listen* to the advice of others but should seek God's wisdom before acting. (Proverbs 15:22; 18:15; and Ephesians 4:14.)
2. *For the envy of others.* This is not within God's plan for the Christian. (Psalms 73:2,3 and Luke 12:15.)
3. *Because it is a game to them.* (Psalms 17:13,14 and Proverbs 13:11.)
4. *For self-esteem.* (I Timothy 6:17 and Revelation 3:17.)
5. *For the love of money.* Again, this is outside God's plan. (I Timothy 6:10 and Hebrews 13:5.)
6. *For protection.* God shows us that we cannot protect ourselves outside of His mercy. (Psalms 50:14,15.)
7. *Because it is their spiritual gift.* (II Corinthians 9:11 and I Timothy 6:17).

How much is enough provision? God indeed asks us to *provide* for our families but not to *protect* them.

1. How much should one provide? Current *provision* for the family. (Proverbs 6:6-11 and Luke 12:30,31.)
2. Should a Christian invest? God not only allows it, but actually directs it for some. (Luke 19:20-26 and II Corinthians 9:10,11.)
3. What about retirement or savings? God admonishes some savings, but allows no hoarding. (Proverbs 21:20 and Luke 12:16-20.)
4. Should a Christian leave an inheritance to his children? Yes, God requires that we provide for our children, even after death, if possible. But for those who cannot, He will never let a godly man's child suffer.

HOW MUCH IS ENOUGH?

(Ecclesiastes 6:3 and Psalms 37:25).

As we look at why people should accumulate wealth, it becomes apparent that *attitude* is foremost in God's plan. But how much can we store and still be within God's plan? In His Word it says, "If I grow rich, I may become content without God" (Proverbs 30:8).

CHAPTER TWELVE

SHARING—GOD'S WAY

Thus far in our study we have reviewed many aspects of God's Word, from an overview of the economy to financial planning. We are now ready to examine a much discussed subject: sharing—from God's perspective.

This study was deliberately delayed until now because it is so intertwined in every other area of finances. Sharing is important, but a Christian should realize that it is only one aspect of God's plan.

God's freedom cannot be experienced in the area of finances unless one:

A. Acknowledges God's ownership over everything and accepts the role of a steward.

B. Surrenders the first part back to God.

C. Seeks the reason that God supplies him a surplus above his own basic needs.

It doesn't matter how diligent, well trained, or know-ledgeable a Christian is, true freedom cannot be experienced unless this area of sharing is under God's control.

We need to dispel some of the religious folklore that has developed in this area also. Christians stand on both sides of the tithing issue. On one side are the legalists who say that unless one tithes, he cannot join the "Christian club." Tithing is sometimes elevated to the exclusion of virtually everything else. The theory is, that once one has established the tithe, spirituality is assured. Such is not the case. Examine what Christ said about some self-righteous men during His time. The Pharisees tithed down to even the last mint leaf in the garden, but they left other things undone — such as living in truth and love (Matthew 23: 23).

On the other side of this issue stand those who believe the tithe is a legalism meant only for the Jew. Therefore, they never establish any goals for tithing or sharing. They give, but on a hit and miss basis. They also are wrong. It is necessary to understand *God's* attitude in this area.

Attitudes cannot be gleaned from a single Scripture verse in most instances. It is necessary to review both Old and New Testament Scriptures to ascertain God's true perspective on sharing, how much to share and with whom to share.

First, let me say that I accept the *entire* Bible as inspired by God, and the lessons given in the Old Testament are as important to us today as those in the New Testament are. "All Scripture is inspired by God and profitable for teaching, for reproof, for correction, for training in righteousness" (II Timothy 3:16).

In many instances Christ clarified certain principles and amplified them for us. Others, He said, were relinquished for a higher authority. For example, it is no longer necessary to make blood sacrifices because Christ said He came to shed His blood once and for all as the ultimate sacrifice. We are no longer slaves to the law because Christ's death pardoned us. But as Paul said, the law didn't make him sin, it *convicted* him of his sin. When God gave the law of tithing, the law didn't *make* the Jews tithe, it showed them where they fell short of what God expected. For a Christian seeking God's will, these principles point the way to peace, happiness and prosperity.

There are many Scriptures dealing with sharing from what God supplies to us. We will look at a few of these to determine God's attitude about the tithe and its applicability today.

How much is the tithe? Is it applicable to the Christian? Why did the Jews tithe? Why is money so important to God that He commands a testimony from it? The answers to these questions are important for us to get straight, lest we fall trap to the folklore around us. I would ask, as you read this section, that you open your mind to the Holy Spirit. Assess what you read on the basis of what *God* says, without any preconceived bias.

The Tithe

The tithe is a very misunderstood area of God's Word. As discussed before, two groups debate this issue; fortunately neither is correct.

God's Word describes the tithe as a *testimony* to God's ownership. It was through the *tithe* that Abraham acknowledged God's ownership. Thus, God was able to direct and prosper him (Genesis 14:20).

If the tithe is a legalism, why did Abraham tithe a tenth of all his spoils back to God? After all, *Abraham had no law.* The written law didn't come until Moses.

Abraham did so because he loved God and was convicted that the tithe belonged to Him. Abraham was a true steward, able to surrender everything, including his most prized possession — Isaac. When God convicted Abraham of the necessity to surrender a tithe, he understood its significance and did so willingly.

In discussing the tithe, the amount is not important to God; He owns *everything.* The amount is important to *us.* The tithe, given as a testimony, reaps a great harvest because it is the seed we plant in God's garden. God is able to take our tithe and multiply it.

Christians often get into discussions about whether one should tithe the gross or the net. I believe that depends on whether you want God to bless your gross or your net. If we are legalistic with God, we can expect the same reward as the Pharisees. If we are loving and generous toward God, God will be loving and generous with us.

Given as a testimony, God promises to prosper it. But God is under absolutely no requirement to return what is given to Him. "Who has first given to Him that it might be paid back to him again?" (Romans 11:35). Uniquely, God promises that if we give out of a true and loving heart, He will return it multiplied.

To find God's will for this area we will look into the Old Testament because it reveals a clear understanding of what the tithe was then and what it is today. Malachi deals with many admonitions about tithing and the blessings of doing so. "Will a man rob God? Yet you are robbing Me! But you say, 'How have we robbed Thee?' In tithes and contributions. You are cursed with a curse, for you are robbing Me, the whole nation of you! 'Bring the whole tithe into the storehouse, so that there may be food in My house, and test Me now in this,' says the Lord of hosts, 'if I will not open for you the windows of heaven, and pour out for you a blessing until there is no more need' " (Malachi 3:8-10).

These words from God are a promise of blessing *and* a warning. God is saying, "Trust Me, bring to Me the full measure of your tithes and offerings that I may open the storehouse for you and give it back. But do not withhold from Me that which I ask."

The amount is not important to God. Paul pointed out in II Corinthians 9:7, that we shouldn't force anyone to give grudgingly, because it's a willing giver that God loves. Give what you believe God has committed *you* to give.

I personally began tithing 10% as a young Christian because I believe this is a *minimum* testimony. And God has blessed that commitment time and time again. I have never seen a Christian give out of love and obedience to God without receiving a blessing.

Deuteronomy 14:23 says, "And you shall eat in the

presence of the Lord your God, at the place where He chooses to establish His name, the tithe of your grain, your new wine, your oil, and the first-born of your herd and your flock, in order that you may learn to fear the Lord your God always."

Why did God establish the tithe? In order *that we may always learn to fear the Lord our God.* Is this applicable today? Review what God's Word says:

"The fear of the Lord is the beginning of wisdom" (Proverbs 9:10). We are looking for ways to be wise with our finances, aren't we? Then we must seek that wisdom from God. One of the ways God said to do it is through tithing.

Sharing Out of Obedience

Many decisions we make in our Christian lives — prehaps even most—do not make sense in relation to what the world believes. Therefore, we make them because of a commitment to God's Word — in other words, out of obedience. A Christian must predetermine that if God defines a course of action in Scripture, he will follow it.

I say this in relation to sharing out of obedience or duty. If we share out of obedience, we do so because God's Word says we are to help others. This attitude begins when we accept the needs of others as our own.

Attitudes play such an important part in sharing with others. Have you ever given to someone but resented it? Well, I have, and almost immediately realized that I had given up more than money. Remember, when you give to meet the needs of others, you give to God.

God *does not* need the money. He is allowing us to share in His work. Anyone that gives willingly receives a blessing that comes only with true love. God will honor your *attitude* more than the amount.

When God places the needs of others on your heart

and you supply those needs, that is obedience. Perhaps it is the need of a Christian organization you are involved with, or perhaps the victims of a natural disaster. You may well be giving to a group that you don't even know, simply out of obedience to God. God will bless the use of your resources for His work.

Get Involved

Be very certain that you are not using a gift of money to avoid a larger responsibility. It may be that God desires your physical involvement as well as financial. In other words, don't just give your money, give of yourself as well.

I know a Christian who is involved with helping to care for the poor in a major city. By caring, he not only gives money, but also gives of himself by establishing thrift shops for the poor in the downtown ghetto areas. These shops supply clothing, furniture, food and other necessities to the poor at prices which they can afford. Although his time is limited, like everyone else's, he does this out of obedience to God and love for others.

He relates that often when he contacts other Christians about helping, the vast majority would rather give a little money to God's work than to get involved personally.

I'd like to emphasize at this point that sharing from obedience differs from the tithe. The tithe is given in recognition of God's ownership (hence, a testimony), while obedience is sharing with others who are in need out of a conviction that they should not do without.

One aspect of God's will can be found in Matthew 25:45: "Then He will answer them, saying, 'Truly I say to you, to the extent that you did not do it to one of the least of these, you did not do it to Me.'" Christ is saying that when He returns He will test the sincerity of our words by the commitment of our resources. This is our duty and obedience—to help those in need because of love for Jesus

Christ.

The other end of the standard is expressed in Matthew 10:42: "And whoever in the name of a disciple gives to one of these little ones even a cup of cold water to drink, truly I say to you he shall not lose his reward." It does not cost much to share water with others. What is Christ saying? *What* you give is not important—not the amount or the value—only the *attitude* with which it is given.

Sharing from Abundance

This is a very difficult area for most of us. In our abundance, the normal tendency is to feel secure and become less involved. As shown before, dangers of abundance are much more subtle than those of poverty.

What is abundance and how can a Christian recognize and acknowledge God's direction? Remember when we were discussing financial planning and living on a budget? The budget helped to establish a surplus and a *plan* for the surplus. That's what the surplus is—our abundance. It is easy to fall trap to feelings of contentment, slipping away from God in our abundance. Many do so because they fear having to share with others. To share from this surplus requires great love; it really means a greater love for God than for money.

Allow me to diverge here a little and discuss giving out of love because it is this principle that makes sharing our abundance possible. Scripture defines at least two levels of love. One is *phileo* and another is *agape.*

Phileo is a brotherly love. It is based on mutual compatability or the sharing of common interests. In other words, it is primarily a love of emotion. When love is given, it is returned; but when the first person withholds love, then, as a result, no love is returned. *Agape* allows one to give love regardless of the response. What the other person does will not really affect me if I am in true *agape* with

God.

Therefore, when we give out of abundance, we cannot give *phileo,* expecting that God will return it. We must give out of *agape,* simply because we love God and expect no reward for that love. To share out of abundance means you have much and want to share with others who need much. Although God has no obligation to return what is given, He wants to do so. Once you have shared out of your abundance, you will find that you cannot out give God. The more you give, the more He multiplies.

One aspect of God's will can be found in I John 3:17, 18, "But whoever has the world's goods, and beholds his brother in need and closes his heart against him, how does the love of God abide in him? Little children, let us not love with word or with tongue, but in deed and truth." Also look into James 2:14-16, "What use is it, my brethren, if a man says he has faith, but he has no works? Can that faith save him? If a brother or sister is without clothing and in need of daily food, and one of you says to them, 'Go in peace, be warmed and be filled'; and yet you do not give them what is necessary for their body; what use is that?"

The other end of God's will can be seen in II Corinthians 8:11,12, "But now finish doing it also, that just as there was the readiness to desire it, so there may be also the completion of it by your ability. For if the readiness is present, it is acceptable according to what a man has, not according to what he does not have." When you give, give out of what you have. Don't worry about what somebody else has to give, or what they are not giving. Give out of the abundance that God has supplied *you.*

Sharing from Sacrifice

Sacrificial giving with a right attitude is possible *only* for those Christians sold out to God. In the United States, giving sacrificially is almost unknown. The attitudes of the world around us have clouded our thinking and dulled our sensitivity to others.

As I said before, God will not allow His work to tarry for lack of funds; He will simply redistribute the necessary funds to Christians who have the correct attitudes—primarily those who are seeking His will and are willing to sacrifice their luxuries for the needs of others.

The use of our money is a very objective measure of our commitment to Jesus Christ and to His work. Christians who bypass God's work because they refuse even a slight discomfort have missed the mark.

When God suggests sacrifice, He does not necessarily mean sacrificing needs. It may mean abandoning some wants and desires as discussed earlier. Perhaps it requires giving up bowling, golfing, eating out or the movies. It may mean foregoing new cars, boats, swimming pools or a larger home.

Sacrificial giving is possible for those who have a little as well as those who have much. All Christians *can* give sacrificially. The best way to begin is by giving up some small part of your plenty for others who have little.

The first generation church set the example for us. They brought their possessions together, pooled them and sold them so that no one would be without. There will come a time in the last generation when this will be a necessity of life. Sharing common ownership by Christians will be the way to survive. We see this pattern in II Corinthians 8:15, "As it is written, 'He who gathered much did not have too much, and he who gathered little had no lack.' "

Today, unfortunately, that concept has been virtually lost. But it is still a viable part of God's plan for the last days. The more that Christians accept the necessity for personal sacrifice, the easier the transition will be.

One reference of God's will concerning sacrifice is found in Luke 3:11, "And he would answer and say to them, 'Let the man who has two tunics share with him who has none;

and let him who has food do likewise.'"Christ considered this a *minimum* sacrifice for those who wished to follow Him—to give, not out of our needs, but from our wants and desires.

His promise for those making sacrifices can be found in Mark 10:29, "Jesus said, 'Truly I say to you, there is no one who has left house or brothers or sisters or mother or father or children or farms, for My sake and for the gospel's sake, but that he shall receive a hundred times as much now in the present age, houses and brothers and sisters and mothers and children and farms, along with persecutions; and in the world to come, eternal life.' "

Christ gave us another reference point when He was standing in the temple, observing the Jews as they came by giving their gifts to the treasury. "And He looked up and saw the rich putting their gifts into the treasury. And He saw a certain poor widow putting in two small copper coins. And He said, 'Truly I say to you, this poor widow put in more than all of them, for they all out of their surplus put into the offering; but she out of her poverty put in all that she had to live on" (Luke 21:1-4).

It is interesting how sacrifice works. Christ said that she put in *more* than all the rest, and yet, it was only two small copper coins. This widow wasn't giving to impress others. Obviously the temple didn't need her pennies, for it was plated with gold and brass, within and without. Nor did she give from her abundance. She gave all that she had because she loved God and obviously felt a bigger need than that of food. She felt the *need* to sacrifice for God.

Sacrifice is an essential attitude for every Christian to adopt. Begin to sacrifice a small portion from your wants or desires for the needs of others. Ask God to lay their needs on your heart. Strive to reflect a difference outside equivalent to the commitment that is inside.

Summary

I hope that at this point in our discussion you now have

the perspective of what sharing means from the Scriptures.

The minimum testimony for any Christian is the *tithe*. A Christian who has never surrendered the tithe to God has never established God's ownership.

We can also share out of *duty* or *obedience* to His Word. Christians must be willing to act out of obedience, not because we understand it, but because it is God's wisdom that we are seeking. To do this requires that we both understand and accept God's Word.

The third step is to share from our *abundance*. It first requires that we establish an abundance by adjusting our standard of living. But once we establish that a surplus exists, it is necessary to *share* rather than store the excess.

Fourth, we can share out of sacrifice. Beginning with some of our wants and desires, we work into a pattern of living that characterizes the life of Christ. If we, who are so mightily blessed, are not willing to sacrifice any of our desires for others, God will simply reallocate the supply to those who are.

CHAPTER THIRTEEN

WHO DESERVES HELP?

There are some important questions all Christians should ask. Who does God direct us to share with? Who is deserving and why? Should we share only with other Christians, or do we have an admonition from God to help non-Christians as well? What about our families? Should a Christian support his church and contribute his entire tithe to it?

As previously stated, it is important in giving that we assess the difference between the needs, wants and desires of others. God has directed us to satisfy the *needs* of others. Whether or not one satisfies the wants or desires of others is an individual decision. This assessment should be made of every individual and organization that asks for assistance.

1. Family Needs.

God requires that we provide for our families. "But if any one does not provide for his own, and especially for those of his household, he has denied the faith, and is worse than an unbeliever " (I Timothy 5:8).

This provision for the family goes beyond just the husband, wife and children. It includes others in the family—mother, father, grandparents, right on down the line. "If any woman who is a believer has dependent widows, let her assist them, and let not the church be burdened, so that it may assist those who are widows indeed" (I Timothy 5:16). This admonition from Paul tells us to support the members of our family. Thus, they will not be a burden on the church (or the government).

Here again, we have seared our consciences, turning these responsibilities over to the government. The government is not adequate to accomplish this task, and government officials neither understand the problems nor have the resources to provide adequately. God wants Christians to provide for their families. What kind of a witness can we be to the non-Christian community if the members of our own families go without? Christians must awaken to this responsibility.

2. Ministering Brethren.

Unfortunately we have also slighted the ministering brethren. It is somehow believed that those in full-time Christian service should live on less than those in the secular world. Why shouldn't a pastor have a comfortable salary? Why shouldn't an evangelist, for instance, live as well as someone who is in business? Do we believe that God's worker is not worthy of an adequate wage?

Review what God says in I Corinthians 9:9, "For it is written in the Law of Moses, 'You shall not muzzle the ox while he is threshing.' God is not concerned about oxen, is He?" And in I Corinthians 9:14, "So also the Lord directed those who proclaim the gospel to get their living from the gospel." And in III John 6,7, "And they bear witness to your love before the church; and you will do well to send them on their way in a manner worthy of God. For they went out for the sake of the Name, accepting nothing from the Gentiles." These references tell us:

A.   The requirement of every Christian is to supply the needs of those ministering God's Word.

B.   We are to send them out in a way worthy of God, *not second class.* I believe a good principle to observe is to pay a pastor as much as the average member of his congregation. If he feels he is overpaid, let it be his responsibility to distribute the surplus.

C. Christians are admonished by God to accept nothing from non-believers but to receive their support from the believers. This admonition must hold equally true of the church; the church should not borrow money from a non-Christian source. Christian organizations should fund their work within the Body of Christ, as John said, "Accepting nothing from the Gentiles" (III John 6,7). How can these needs be met unless Christians accept this responsibility to supply the ministering brethren?

3. Christian Community.

Care for the Christian community. "Honor widows who are widows indeed" (I Timothy 5:3). The directive that Paul gave for "widows indeed" concerns those who have no family to support them. Therefore, the burden of support is placed on the church; and the *church* is to supply their needs.

How many churches really do this today? How many congregations in the United States have, as a regular part of their budget, money to supply the needs of Christians in their church who cannot make their own way? That applies to those who are temporarily out of work, to the injured or disabled and to the elderly.

I believe it is an abomination before God to see widows in the Christian community depending on welfare for their support. If they are qualified and have established themselves accordingly, it is a direct requirement from God to the church to care for them.

Here is also the key to where our tithe goes. In God's plan, the Church (body of believers) is to administer the tithe and distribute it to the needs of the body. Unfortunately, not all churches adhere to this plan. I believe that if a church observes God's plan, both teaching His

Word and administering His money, then all of the tithe should be placed in its care. However, if the church ignores its physical responsibilities, then each Christian must vote his own conviction. Under no circumstances can the qualified needy be ignored. Christ gave this admonition to the Pharisees in Matthew 15:5,6: "But you say, 'Whoever shall say to his father or mother, "Anything of mine you might have been helped by has been given to God," he is not to honor his father or his mother. And thus you invalidated the word of God for the sake of your tradition."

So long as you receive teaching from the church you must provide the needs of its workers. If the church does not understand God's plan, you should work diligently to help them do so. If you find a closed attitude in this area, I would recommend changing to a place of worship compatible with your commitment where you can entrust God's wealth.

4. *Non-Christian Community.*

We are also *directed* to share with the non-Christian community. When God talks specifically about the "believer," the "elect" or the "Body of Christ," He is referring to Christians. Other Scriptures that deal with sharing but do not refer directly to the Body of Christ are intended to include the non-Christian community.

I have found that the preponderance of Scripture deals with supplying the needs of the non-Christian community. Perhaps 10 times as many references pertain to sharing with non-believers as opposed to only Christians. It is obvious that God set up absolute standards:

a. That we are not to accept resources from the non-Christian.

b. That we are to be a witness to them through our readiness to share.

Matthew 5:42 states, "Give to him who asks of you, and do not turn away from him who wants to borrow from you." Matthew 10:42: "And whoever in the name of a disciple gives to one of these little ones even a cup of cold water to drink, truly I say to you he will not lose his reward." Neither of these Scriptures, as well as 50-odd others, deal *only* with Christians. They deal with the community at large, both believers and non-believers.

We are to be witnesses to non-Christians through our material resources, demonstrating that Christ, not money, is ruling our lives. Commitment in Christianity is often related to whether one is more committed to money than the needs of others. Upon this principle Christ based much of His teaching, such as in Luke 12:33, "Sell your possessions and give to charity; make yourselves purses which do not wear out, an unfailing treasure in heaven, where no thief comes near, nor moth destroys."

I would invite everyone reading this study to stop at this point. Bow your head and ask God to relieve you of the burden of worry and anxiety and frustration surrounding money. Ask that He would place on your heart only those people that you are able to help. *Believe* that God is going to give you the ability as well as the responsibility to do so. Commit yourself right now to becoming a Christian witness in this area of giving in the name of our Lord.

Evaluate the Recipient

A Christian should be very sensitive, not only concerning whom he assists, but how the money is used.

What about the myriad of individuals and organizations who approach us? How can you assess whether they are doing God's work?

God has established the requirements for us. The standards are clear for individuals—assess whether they are willing and able to work. Also are they asking for needs, or wants and desires. Do not give to just anybody who asks but get involved with them personally if possible.

Share God's principles of finance with them. Help them establish a budget and live by it. Find out *how* they are living. Would they consume the money you might give them in alcohol? Are they consuming their present income in foolishness? If so, you have no requirement to support them. In fact, by doing so you may well be interfering in God's plan for them.

Christian organizations should be assesed in a like manner. Not only does God provide opportunities for giving to the needs of the saints but also to invest tithes, offerings and sacrifices into His work. Unfortunately, today in our society Christians are besieged by charitable requests from every side. From every corner of the earth, organizations come. Many are deserving, but some are poorly managed, unfruitful and even dishonest. Seek God's wisdom *before* giving. Get literature from them that thoroughly describes the organization and its doctrine. Talk to others who have invested. Require references if you have never heard of the group before. Let the organization know *why* you are questioning them. Be discerning, be a good steward of God's resources. A minimum check list would be:

A. Is the organization communicating the true message of Jesus Christ? If they are not, do not get involved with them. This refers to organizations that come in the name of Christ. There are other charitable organizations that do great work through secular channels.

B. Are people responding to the organization positively? Are lives being changed as a result of their input?

C. Is the organization seeking and accomplishing goals? If so, they should be able to explain their goals to you.

D. Are the lives of those in leadership positions consistent with the scriptural principles that God outlines for Christian organizations?

E. Is the organization multiplying itself, or is it dying out? (This is not always an absolute standard because you may find new leadership in an organization that is seeking to expand previous boundaries.) Ask around and be discerning. Pay a visit to them personally, particularly if the decision involves a large amount of money.

F. Is there a standard of excellence along with a freedom from lavishness and waste? How much money do they spend raising money? If you find an organization spending half or more of its finances in order to raise more money, I would question their effectiveness. Can you invest elsewhere and get better return for God's money?

G. Check them out with other Christian organizations. If you know other Christian organizations that you trust, ask them. Tell them you are looking for an *honest* answer.

In summary, share willingly according to God's plan but be discerning and cautious as a steward. Accept nothing less than excellence for the Lord's money.

CHAPTER FOURTEEN

FINANCIAL BREATHING

In this section we are going to amplify some of the pre-viously stated concepts, particularly those that will help you understand how to make financial decisions by God's plan. The principles presented are practical and applicable and can be traced back to one or more of the scriptural concepts that have previously been given.

I recall, looking back on my Christian growth, that one of the most important concepts I ever heard was that of spiritual breathing. This concept is taken from I John 1:9: "If we confess our sins, He is faithful and righteous to forgive us our sins and to cleanse us from all unrighteousness." An examination of this Scripture shows that a sequence of spiritual events occurs:

    a.   God convicts us of our sins.

    b.   We acknowledge them and ask forgiveness.

    c.   God cleanses us and forgives our transgressions.

Another important point to remember is that God will convict us and Satan will condemn us. Once our sins are cleansed and restitution made (if God so declares), He no longer remembers them.

What a great relief it was for me to understand this. Because, for the first few months after accepting Christ, I went about trying to make myself into the kind of Christian that I thought God wanted me to be. After struggling unsuccessfully, I found myself totally inadequate. No matter how hard I tried, I could not overcome my past. I had few victories over the burdens that kept me shackled.

I shared my frustration with a Christian friend and his reply was, "Really makes you feel inferior, doesn't it?" To which I answered, "Amen!" Then he said, "Someone who struggles trying to make himself into a Christian quickly develops an inferiority complex. But it's not all that complex, because we really are inferior."

None of us is adequate to make ourselves into the kind of Christian that God wants us to be. Why? Because God cannot tolerate sin in a life. And all of us have sinned. We sinned before we came to God, and we will sin as Christians. The concept of spiritual breathing tells us to exhale the bad air and inhale the good air.

All that was required was to confess my sin, exhaling the bad air, and appropriate the fullness of the Holy Spirit, inhaling the good air. What a change it made in my life! There was a freedom that I had never experienced before. It gave me the ability to put the things of the past in the past and to start afresh with God from that point.

Be careful not to adulterate the concept of spiritual breathing. Forgiveness does not provide us with a license to sin and expect forgiveness, because if there is no *changed attitude,* there can be *no* forgiveness. But when there is a changed attitude, God says He will forgive us. As I thought about this in relation to finances, I realized that we as

FINANCIAL BREATHING

Christians can appropriate the forgiveness that God promises in the area of finances, too.

I'd like to share how you, as a Christian, can *breathe financially:*

1. Acknowledge God's Ownership Daily.

Be certain that each and every day the affairs and decisions of that day are surrendered to God. Since problems are day-by-day occurrences, our acknowledgment of God's authority and His forgiveness should be daily as well. Each day must begin with a clean heart, meaning that we have no unconfessed sin in our lives.

What are the essential elements in making sound financial decisions? Adequate knowledge and the wisdom to apply it. "The fear of the Lord is the beginning of knowledge; fools despise wisdom and instruction" (Proverbs 1: 7). Thus it is vital in financial breathing to recognize that it is God's knowledge and wisdom that you are seeking.

To do so you *must* surrender *every* decision to God. "So you will find favor and good repute in the sight of God and man. Trust in the Lord with all your heart, and do not lean on your own understanding. In all your ways acknowledge Him, and He will make your paths straight" (Proverbs 3:4-6).

Then apply the discipline taught in Luke 9:23, "If anyone wishes to come after Me, let him deny himself, and take up his cross *daily,* and follow Me."

2. Accept God's Direction.

Once you have surrendered control of your finances to God, accept His judgment. Do not precondition your response by expecting only *increases.*

Paul said he had learned to abase and to abound, but in all things to give thanks. So after you have surrendered decision-making to God, accept His wisdom.

The adversities that are faced may be God using you as a testimony for other people or reinforcing a lesson. I have often heard, and found it to be true in my own life, that during times of trial we grow the most. God says that it is through fire that silver is purified.

Don't seek escape from difficulties, seek peace during them. "Be anxious for nothing, but in everything by prayer and supplication with thanksgiving let your requests be made known to God" (Philippians 4:6). In every decision trust that God guides your direction. Verify your decisions by checking against the Lord's Word, confirming them in prayer and accepting His answer.

There is one final step in accepting God's decisions and that is found in I Thessalonians 5:18: "In everything give thanks; for this is God's will for you in Christ Jesus." When you ask God for a decision, and He complies, thank Him for it, whether or not it is the one you were looking for.

There are many real life examples of this principle. For instance, at one point I counseled a couple having financial difficulties. Their income was not sufficient to meet their wants, and they had drifted into financial bondage.

In reviewing the circumstances with the husband, I found that he was not really satisfied in his work. It seems this company was not dealing fairly with him because of his Christian commitment. As a result of this his witness was hindered in dealing with customers. In our discussion, I asked him if he was committed to seeking God's wisdom and not man's. He replied, "Yes, I am." I then asked him if he was willing to surrender the decision on his employment back to God and let Him decide the next step. After we prayed about it, he again reaffirmed his commitment to God's will no matter what it was.

He prayed for two things: that God would provide a definite direction concerning his work and would relieve him of his debt. God worked specifically on both of these points. First, he was convicted to confront his employers concerning their attitude about his religious beliefs. They declared that they no longer had a place for him in their employ and dismissed him. Upon termination, they surrendered the money that was due him in a savings plan. That money was sufficient to pay off all his debts.

Although it was not the method we might have chosen, he thanked God for the answer. Indeed, God's answer was *very* specific, for he was removed from a position that was not honoring to God and his debts were cleared at the same time.

More Christians should learn to accept God's wisdom when they ask for it. God loves us deeply, and He will never give us less than the very best for our lives.

3. Establish the Tithe.

As previously defined, give God the *first* part of your income as a testimony of His ownership. "Give, and it will be given to you; good measure, pressed down, shaken together, running over, they will pour into your lap. For whatever measure you deal out to others, it will be dealt to you in return" (Luke 6:38). This is an essential step in financial breathing. Not only do we surrender our decisions to God and accept His leading, but then we surrender back to God a minimum testimony of His ownership.

The tithe is a *spiritual* investment and cannot be evaluated on the basis of profit and loss. Too many Christians look at tithing in worldly terms. But God is the only business manager in existence who can make 90% go farther than 100%.

4. Sacrifice.

As previously discussed, the concept of sacrifice is not

very popular with most Christians or Christian organizations. Most of us like to discuss this area in glowing generalities rather than specifics. It's all right for the pastor to mention sacrifice in terms of missionaries or full-time Christians, but when he talks about giving up golf or a new car for God's work, suddenly he is a radical.

Many Christians have been asked to sacrifice their lives, while others around the world sacrifice the needs of everyday life to deliver God's Word. But for most of us, sacrificing amounts only to delaying or eliminating a few desires.

Those who have truly surrendered their finances to God have also experienced His faithfulness. "And everyone who has left houses or brothers or sisters or father or mother or children or farms for My name's sake, shall receive many times as much, and shall inherit eternal life" (Matthew 19: 29).

God provides many opportunities to invest in the lives of others in need. I recall a story a Christian friend related one time of such an opportunity. Bob lived in a middle-class suburb and for several months the neighbor in back had been the source of much conflict. Though both were professing Christians, neither was willing to admit that he could possibly be wrong.

They argued about fences, dogs, trash cans and many other things to the point that they no longer had communication. Just to cap off the whole issue, his neighbor moved some chicken coops into his back yard housing about a dozen chickens. At this point the cold war got hot. Bob said he just knew that his

neighbor got those chickens to irritate him. Every time he went into his back yard and heard or saw those chickens he grew more irritated.

Bob got nastier and nastier with his neighbor until finally his own Christian witness deteriorated to nothing. In the depths of despair, he was convicted that he was in the wrong and should make it right with his brother. Going to his neighbor's house, he knocked at the door. As his neighbor answered, Bob told him, "I'm sorry that I've been so obnoxious; it's my fault and I ask your forgiveness." Immediately accepting the apology, his neighbor thanked him and asked him in.

As they began to talk, it became apparent why the Lord had been convicting Bob. Several months before, this neighbor and his wife had been in an automobile accident. His wife had been injured and was still disabled. He had had several vertebrae in his back fractured and was unable to work. Being self-employed, he drew no income at all. For several months they lived off their savings, but with the doctors' bills and living expenses, their finances had been totally depleted. When he moved the chickens into his back yard, it was not an attempt to irritate his neighbors but an effort to have food to eat. Bob said he broke down and cried and asked his neighbor to forgive him for being so callous.

As a result, a bond of friendship grew in which one Christian was able to help meet the needs of another. Bob also said it was a great blessing to no longer see those chickens in the back yard!

This is just another case of being aware and sensitive to the needs of others. It is amazing, when you allow yourself to be sensitive, how painless a personal sacrifice then becomes. Without personal contact this sensitivity becomes more remote and less apparent.

Thus if a Christian wants to give God control of his finances, he must:

1. Daily surrender to God every financial decision, no

matter how large or how small.

2. Accept God's wisdom for every decision.
3. Give the minimum testimony to God of His owner-ship.
4. Willingly seek to share with other people, even if it requires a sacrifice to do so.

CHAPTER FIFTEEN

PRINCIPLES OF FINANCIAL DECISION-MAKING

How can a Christian make financial decisions according to God's plan? By understanding His directives. Every decision requires a thorough understanding of God's attitudes, and that understanding comes as a result of reading God's Word and communicating with Him.

One who never prays, or never listens while praying, cannot hear God speak through prayer. Just as one who never reads God's Word cannot hear God speak through Scripture. If a Christian never asks God's direction on an investment or a financial decision, he will never get an answer.

The principles for financial decisions summarized here are the do's and don'ts on how God would have us manage money.

1. Avoid Speculation.

Every Christian should seek God's increase and make no provision for speculative schemes. Many times these enticing programs are not only unethical but also border on the fringes of being unlawful. Included in these are pyramid franchising systems, multi-level marketing systems, unregistered stock offers and scores of other questionable ventures.

You should assess *every* "opportunity" in relation to your own commitment to Christ. As previously discussed, *do not* let others make your financial decisions for you. We are not to be as children, changing our minds just because somebody comes up with a new idea. Make *your* decisions in light of your goals; evaluate whether it is necessary that you get into a venture.

Often the result of involvement in speculative schemes will be a loss of your witness, a loss of your credibility and a loss of your money. So take God's advice and *avoid* them. "A man with an evil eye hastens after wealth, and does not know that want will come upon him" (Proverbs 28:22). Sound like anybody you know?

Money that may take years to save can be lost in an instant. Even worse is the compromise of a Christian who has talked others into the same dumb trap. "Do not weary yourself to gain riches, cease from your consideration of it. When you set your eyes on it, it is gone. For wealth certainly makes itself wings, like an eagle that flies toward the heavens" (Proverbs 23:4,5).

You must precondition your attitudes to avoid speculative "opportunities." The temptation of easy money and the emotionalism of its sponsors will sorely test your commitment. But, remember, Satan doesn't have to attack in a "spiritual" area if he gets a foothold in your finances, because that will soon affect you spiritually.

2 Keep Your Finances Current.

The second principle of financial decision-making is to always manage your finances on a current basis. In other words, make no provision in your financial planning to borrow money beyond your ability to repay, even for one day. Many Christians have become involved in investment programs they could not afford and borrowed money to invest where repayment was dependent on a future event. To do so is to flirt with financial disaster.

If what you buy jeopardizes your future financial freedom, forget it. Impulse buying, either for investment or consumption, is disastrous. When you evaluate a purchase, investment or otherwise, consider the obligation in light of *known income.*

Certainly this is a conservative attitude, but this philosophy is directed toward long-range peace not short-range profit. "For which one of you, when he wants to build a tower, does not first sit down and calculate the cost, to see if he has enough to complete it? Otherwise, when he has laid a foundation, and is not able to finish, all who observe it begin to ridicule him, saying, 'This man began to build and was not able to finish' " (Luke 14:28,29). Plan for tomorrow by prudence today; make your plans in light of present circumstances not on some future event.

James 4:13,14 advises us, "Come now, you who say, 'Today or tomorrow, we shall go to such and such a city, and spend a year there and engage in business and make a profit.' Yet you do not know what your life will be like tomorrow. You are just a vapor that appears for a little while and then vanishes away."

Maintain the principle of staying debt free; make *every* decision on the basis of whether it may ultimately result in bondage.

3. Consider Your Witness.

Consider every decision on the basis of its effect on the work and reputation of Christ. Do not put God into a financial corner and place Him in the role of a "bailer"; I suspect that God does not like to sit in the back of a leaky boat and continually have to bail us out. We are told in I Corinthians 10:31, "Whether, then, you eat or drink or whatever you do, do all to the glory of God."

To launch out on feelings, even in doing God's work, and then to depend on God to bail you out is *not* according to His plan. Christians in full-time ministry should accept this as one of the basic financial decisions for doing God's work. If one must borrow outside of God's people in order to do His work, beware! That is not according to His plan. "The rich rules over the poor, and the borrower becomes the lender's slave" (Proverbs 22:7).

God *will not* frustrate His work for lack of money, neither will He place a Christian organization in servitude to a secular institution.

This same principle applies to a different area, dealing unethically with others. As stated earlier, there are *no* small lies or small thefts. There are only liars and thieves.

If you deal unfairly or unethically with someone else, then it is *your* witness that will suffer. Establish this principle firmly in your heart that no matter what, you will tell the *whole truth* to the best of your ability. There is no simple way to accomplish this, for frequently, at just the time you are most vulnerable, an "opportunity" will arise. If you stumble, make restitution and admit your error. God will honor your commitment.

4. Give to the Needs of Others.

Avoid *lending* to another person in need where *giving* is possible. Why? If someone in need approaches you for a loan, you are much better off to give. The witness and fellowship this provides is lasting while the temporary gratitude of a loan quickly fades.

I recall reading an article in which the question was asked: "What is a distant relative?" The answer: "It is a close relative you loan money to." Unfortunately, the same thing is often true with Christians. What is a distant Christian friend? It is a close Christian friend to whom you loaned money.

If someone approaches you for financial help in acquiring wants or desires, then you should question whether to supply them at all. But if they are in need and on your heart, you have a responsibility from God to supply that need.

PRINCIPLES OF FINANCIAL DECISION-MAKING

II Corinthians 9:13 says, "Because of the proof given by this ministry they will glorify God for your obedience to your confession of the gospel of Christ, and for the liberality of your contribution to them and to all." *Give* to the needs of others and have them glorify God because of the proof of your faith.

5. *Never Co-sign.*

Co-signing means to pledge your assets against the debts of someone else. Scripture specifically forbids this whenever it speaks of "surety" or "striking of hands." There are many references to this in Proverbs.

It is interesting to note that Solomon, king and ruler of Israel, wrote much about not co-signing. It seems obvious that time after time lenders came before him collecting co-signed debts, taking every possession from those who co-signed. He noted how ridiculous that was, saying, Friend, they'll not only take your house, they'll take your bed with it. "A man of great anger shall bear the penalty, for if you rescue him, you'll only have to do it again" (Proverbs 19:19).

This concept goes beyond personal co-signing. It also applies to business co-signing. If you work for a company and consistently co-sign notes (with the possible exception of a privately-held business), you are also violating this principle.

"My son, if you have become surety for your neighbor, have given a pledge for a stranger, if you have been snared with the words of your mouth, have been caught with the words of your mouth, do this then, my son, and deliver yourself; since you have come into the hand of your neighbor, go, humble yourself, and importune your neighbor" (Proverbs 6:1-3).

Of all the areas of Scripture, this would seem to be one of the most explicit. Yet, we continually violate this principle and rationalize it with human logic. Ask any banker what type of loans he considers the most likely to default and practically everyone will say, co-signed notes. Not only is co-signing a violation of the principle of surety, but by doing so, the co-signer may be interfering with God's plan for someone else.

I have come to the absolute conclusion in my life that when God makes a principle clear, I should obey it, not question it.

6. Avoid Indulgence.

Discern the difference in every purchase made between needs, wants and desires. This applies not only to purchases of material goods, but investments as well. Before you invest, discern *why* you are investing. Is it to help you fulfill a need? Is it to help you further God's work. Or is it to satisfy a hungry ego? What will you do with the money if God multiplies it?

If you believe the purchase is within God's will, peace will be a by-product. But, if you assess that the purchase is a desire or a whim, stop, recheck God's principles again. Many Christians are frustrated because they cannot distinguish between luxuries and necessities. Consequently, they seek fulfillment through the same channels as non-Christians and then wonder why they have a fruitless Christian walk.

I believe that God wants us to live comfortably. But He does not want us to live *lavishly.*

At a time when our resources could be used to promote God's work throughout the world, we should evaluate every financial motive. "Do not love the world, nor the things in the world. If any one loves the world, the love of the Father is not in him. For all that is in the world, the lust of the flesh and the lust of the eyes and the boastful pride of life, is not from the Father, but is from the world" (I John 2:15,16).

7. Prepare for Decreases.

Being prepared for unexpected decreases in funds is a vital part of keeping current. When you make a financial decision, consider what would happen if you had even a small decrease in funds.

This is especially important when the wife works and expenses are incurred assuming two incomes are guaranteed. What if you are forced to reduce your income? Are you prepared to adjust as necessary to live within your means? What if God asks you to do something in His work that requires a reduced income? Can you do so? To the Christian who is totally trusting in Christ moment by moment, the quality of life is independent of the circumstances, as Paul states in Philippians 4:12,13: "I know how to get along with humble means, and I also know how to live in prosperity; in any and every circumstance I have learned the secret of being filled and going hungry, both of having abundance and suffering need. I can do all things through Him who strengthens me."

Do not operate at the upper limit of your income, but make your financial decisions in light of the fact that you may need to reduce your level of living. The ability to thank God in every circumstance demonstrates full dependence and trust in Him.

8. If You Don't Have Peace, Don't Buy.

Often we are not responsive enough to God's Word or to His presence to hear Him except through that inner turmoil known as a *lack of peace.* As a last resort God will use this to provide direction. Accordingly, *if you do not have peace, do not get involved.* If a quick decision is required, do not get involved. Take the time to think and to pray about it; perhaps God has alternative provision for you.

Many times I have made decisions on the spur of the moment. There are very few of those decisions that I have not later regretted. Pre-set in your mind clearly the principle that you *will not* make a decision under pressure. You may miss a few "good deals," but you will also miss a great many bad ones. "It is the blessing of the Lord that makes rich, and He adds no sorrow to it" (Proverbs 10:22).

Become sensitive to God's inner guidance; He will

166

always provide direction if you are seeking it. Even when we fail to see the right path clearly in God's Word or fail to hear it in prayer, God will place an unrest inside that will keep us out of financial bondage.

Summary

Principles of Financial Breathing:
1. Acknowledge God's ownership daily (Proverbs 3:4-6).
2. Accept God's direction (I Thessalonians 5:18).
3. Establish the tithe (Luke 6:38).
4. Seek self-sacrifice (Luke 3:11).

Principles of Financial Decision-making:
1. Avoid speculation (Proverbs 28:22).
2. Keep your finances current (Luke 14:28,29).
3. Consider your witness (I Corinthians 10:31).
4. Give to the needs of others (II Corinthians 9:13).
5. Never co-sign (Proverbs 19:19).
6. Avoid indulgence (I Timothy 6:8).
7. Prepare for decreases (Philippians 4:12,13).
8. Seek God's peace (Proverbs 10:22).

This concludes our study of God's financial principles. I would like to challenge you to pray concerning how God would have you specifically change your lifestyle as a result of the concepts you have learned.

PART III
USING GOD'S PLAN

CHAPTER 16

PRACTICAL APPLICATIONS

In most books a great deal of information is presented that would be extremely valuable if applied, but, unfortunately, it is seldom put into practice. As a friend once told me, information without application leads to frustration. To help avoid that common problem, in this section you will find ideas to assist you in applying God's principles of finance.

Each area should be carefully and prayerfully considered and then acted upon. Some of the specifics, such as a family budget, may seem rudimentary, but unless the basic areas are under control, the more complex ones cannot be.

Family Financial Planning

1. Family Communication Goals.
Communication is vital to family financial planning. To enhance that communication, some questions are listed below for both husband and wife. I suggest that each of you do them separately. Write down every answer as if your spouse were asking the question. Then, during a time when you won't be interrupted, evaluate these together. Begin your evaluation by praying about your

168

PRACTICAL APPLICATIONS

time together, opening your hearts to the Holy Spirit.

The questions are intended to enrich the discussions of mature, communicating Christian couples. They are not intended to become an additional source of friction for couples totally void of communication. Use them as tools of love, not ammunition for war.

A. PERSONAL GOALS.

To be answered as if your (husband) (wife) were asking:

1. What are your personal goals in life?

_____

2. What personal goals have you set for this coming year?

_____

3. How can I help you achieve your goals?

_____

4. What can I do to help or improve our financial situation?

_____

5. Do you feel there is a proper balance between my outside activity and my time at home?

_____

6. Would you like me to do more things around the house such as cleaning, decorating, etc.?

_____

7. In regard to my activities outside the home, what would you consider as priorities?

_____

PRACTICAL APPLICATIONS

8. Do you feel I need to improve in any area, such as the way I dress, my appearance, manners, attitudes?

_____

B. MARRIAGE GOALS.

1. Do you believe that our marriage is maturing and that we are coming closer together?

_____

2. Do you feel that we clearly communicate with each other?

_____

3. Do you feel that I am sensitive to your personal needs?

_____

4. What would you like me to say or do the next time you seem to be angry with me or you are not speaking to me?

_____

5. The next time you are late in getting ready to go some place, what would you like me to say or do?

_____

6. What would you like me to do or say the next time you seem to be getting impatient with something or someone?

_____

7. What would you like me to say or do if you begin to criticize someone?

_____

8. Do you feel I need to improve in getting ready on time or getting to meetings on time?

_____

9. Do you feel we should go out together more often?

_____

10. Do I make cutting remarks about you or criticize you in front of other people?

_____

11. What should I do in public to encourage you?

_____

12. Do I respond to your suggestions and ideas as if I had already thought of them instead of thanking you and encouraging you to contribute more?

_____

13. Do I tell you enough about what I do every day?

_____

14. What little acts of love do I do for you?

_____

15. What most often causes you to get angry with me?

_____

16. Do I convey my admiration and respect often enough?

_____

17. Do we "play act" a happy marriage in front of other people?

_____

PRACTICAL APPLICATIONS

18. What do you think I Corinthians 7:3-7 means?

_____

19. Do you feel we need to see a marriage counselor?

_____

20. What are the responsibilities of a "help-mate"?

_____

21. Do we give each other the same attention we did before we had children?

_____

C. FAMILY GOALS.

1. What are our family goals?

_____

2. Are we achieving our family goals?

_____

3. a. (Wife only) What can I do to help you fulfill your responsibilities as spiritual leader of our family?

_____

    b. (Husband only) How can I better fulfill my responsibilities as spiritual leader?

_____

4. Do you feel we are meeting the spiritual needs of of our family?

_____

5. What kinds of family devotions should we have?

_____

172

PRACTICAL APPLICATIONS

6. List the responsibilities stated for the husband and wife in the following passages:

   I Peter 3:1,2 _____

   Colossians 3:18,19_____

   I Timothy 2:11-15_____

   I Corinthians 11:3_____

   Ephesians 5:17-33_____

7. Do you feel we have a consistent prayer life together?

   _____

8. Do you feel we are adequately involved in our local church?

   _____

9. Do you feel we are meeting the physical needs of our family?

   _____

10. Should we improve our eating habits?

   _____

11. Should we get more exercise?

   _____

12. Do we make good use of our time? For example, do we watch too much TV? Should we have more hobbies? Read more?

   _____

13. How and when shall we discipline our children? What do you think the biblical viewpoint of discipline is?

_____

14. On a sheet of paper, list the responsibilities of parents and their children in the following passages:

Colossians 3:20,21_____

Hebrews 12:5-11_____

Proverbs 3:11, 12_____

Ephesians 6:4_____

15. What kind of instruction and training should we be giving to our children in the home?

_____

D. FINANCIAL GOALS.

1. Do you think I handle money properly?

_____

2. What suggestions do you have for how I can manage our money better?

_____

3. Do you think I am:
   A.   Too frugal? _____
   B.   Too extravagant?_____
   C.   About right?_____
   Why?_____

PRACTICAL APPLICATIONS

4. Do you think I accept financial responsibilities well?

   _____

5. Do you think we communicate financial goals well?

   _____

6. What is your immediate financial goal?

   _____

7. What is your primary goal for this year?

   _____

8. What is your plan for our children's education?

   _____

9. What is your retirement goal?

   _____

10. What do you think about tithing?
    A. Is tithing necessary? _____
    B. How much?_____
    C. Where should it go?_____
11. How do you feel about *giving* in general?

    _____

12. Do you like the way we live?

    _____

13. What changes would you like to see?

    _____

II. The Family Budget.
   Why is a budget necessary?

175

PRACTICAL APPLICATIONS

A. To help those who are not living within their means to do so.
B. To help those with a potential surplus to fix their level of expenses.
C. To help establish a reasonable level of living for those who want to do so.

The initial tendency is to create an unrealistic budget, one that makes no provision for variables like clothes, dentists, doctors, entertainment, etc. To do so will only frustrate your efforts, cause your budget to fail and cause you and your spouse to lose confidence in budgeting.

The next tendency is to create a budget—and then stop! There is no magic in a budget; it is only a written expression of what you must do to be a good steward. Action is required to make it work, and you may need to make sacrifices to live within your budget.

Two budgets are actually necessary. The first determines your present status. The second determines your goals (a budget based on spendable income). If you are really serious about being the best steward possible, then a budget is necessary. But, no amount of *intention* is effective without action.

Steps to Making a Budget.
In making and using a budget, there are several logical steps, each requiring individual effort. A sample form for budgeting is shown in figure 1. Use this form to guide your budget preparation.

Step 1 — *List Expenditures in the Home on a Monthly Basis.*
A. *Fixed Expenses* — These include the following:

- Tithe
- Federal income taxes (if taxes are deducted, ignore this item)

176

- State income taxes (if taxes are deducted, ignore this item)
- Federal Social Security taxes (if taxes are deducted, ignore this item).
- Housing expense (payment/rent)
- Residence taxes
- Residence insurance
- Other

B.   *Variable Expenses.*

- Food
- Outstanding debts
- Utilities
- Insurance (life, health, auto)
- Entertainment, recreation
- Clothing allowance
- Medical - dental
- Savings
- Miscellaneous

  NOTE: In order to accurately determine variable expenses, it is suggested that both husband and wife keep an expense diary for 30 days. List *every* expenditure, even quarter purchases.

Step 2 – *List Available Income per Month.*

  NOTE: If you operate on a non-fixed monthly income, use a yearly average divided into months.

- Salary
- Rents
- Notes
- Interest
- Dividends

PRACTICAL APPLICATIONS

- — Income tax refund
- — Other

Step 3 — *Compare Income vs. Expenses.*

If total income exceeds total expenses, you have only to implement a method of budget control in your home. If, however, expenses exceed income (or more stringent controls in spending are desired), additional steps are necessary. In that case, an analysis of each budget area to reduce expenses is called for. These areas are outlined below.

Budget Problems Analysis

A.   *Bookkeeping Errors* — In order to maintain an orderly budget it is necessary to keep records. This includes both the previously established home budget and adequate bank records. Many people fail to exercise any control over checking accounts and seldom or never balance their records. It is *impossible* to balance a home budget without balancing your checking account. Go to your bank account manager and ask his help if you cannot balance your records. Some helpful hints for this area are:
1. Use a ledger type checkbook (as opposed to a stub type).
2. List all check numbers before writing the *first* check.
3. Record *every* check in the ledger immediately, in detail.
4. Only one person should keep the ledger and checkbook.
5. Balance the ledger *every* month.

B.   *Hidden Debts* — These include bills that may not come due on a monthly basis. Nevertheless your budget must provide for reduction of these items; failure to do

PRACTICAL APPLICATIONS

so will only frustrate your efforts to be a good steward.

Some debts of this type might include:
1. Record companies, books, magazines, etc.
2. Retail outlet stores credit.
3. Family, friends.
4. Doctor, dentist, etc.
5. Taxes.
6. Yearly insurance premiums.

C.   *Impulse Items* — As mentioned in an earlier section, impulse buying is common to most of us. Unfortunately, credit cards have provided the means to buy beyond the means to repay (to the sacrifice of other needs).

A list of impulse purchases can range from homes, cars and expensive trips to tools and entertainment items. The value is not the issue; its necessity is. Consider every purchase in light of your budgeted items and avoid buying anything on impulse.

Some hints to reduce impulse buying:
1. Use a delayed purchase plan. (Buy nothing that is outside your budget unless you wait for 30 days.)
2. During those 30 days, determine to find at least two items similar to the one you want to purchase to compare prices.
3. Allow only one new purchase at a time that is not part of your planned budget.
4. *Never* use credit cards for impulse purchases.
5. Stay out of the stores.

D.   *Gifts* — These items can jeopardize a budget quickly. It is unfortunate that in our society we tend to place more emphasis on the gift than the giver, and too many times busy parents substitute expensive gifts for personal involvement with their children. Begin to seek

179

alternatives for costly gifts both within the family and with friends. Regardless of your financial status, determine to bring this area under control. The following are some hints:

1. Keep an event calendar during the year and plan ahead.
2. Initiate some *family* crafts and *make* the gifts you need. For example: wall plaques, knickknacks, purses, string art, etc. Not only do these make good gifts, but they reflect effort and love.
3. Draw family names for selected gifts rather than each family member giving to everyone.
4. Do not buy gifts on credit.
5. Help your children *earn* money for gifts.
6. Send cards on special birthdays and anniversaries.

Budget Busters

"Budget busters" are the large potential problem areas that can ruin a budget. Failure to control even one of these problems can result in financial disaster in the home. This area is evaluated by *typical* budget percentages for a $12,000-$18,000 income. Naturally, these percentages are not absolute and will vary with income and geographical location.

A.   *Housing* (26% of net income).

Typically, this is one of the largest home budget problems. Many families buy a home they can't afford, motivated by peer pressure or some other pressure. It is *not* necessary for everyone to *own* a home. The decision to buy or rent should be based on needs and financial ability rather than internal or external pressure.

The following are some hints to observe:

1. Purchase a home only if the total payments (mortgage, taxes, insurance, etc.) do not exceed 30% of

your net income.
2. Do not finance a second mortgage for the down payment.
3. Consider the monthly upkeep of a home. This usually averages 10% of the monthly payment.
4. Consider the tax deduction for interest paid as a reduction in monthly payment.
5. If trading, consider whether you *need* to do so.

B. *Food* (24% of net income).
Many families buy too much food. Others buy too little. Typically, the average American family buys the wrong type of food. The reduction of a family's food bill requires quantity and quality planning.

Perhaps one of the best ways to plan food purchases is to decide on your daily menu *first*. Once you have established what your family is to eat, then select the various ingredients. Few homemakers take the time and effort to actually plan and write out family menus, but once the habit is developed, its benefits are obvious. Grocery shopping ceases to be a hunt-and-find weekly expedition; it becomes another step in financial planning.

Hints on grocery shopping:
— Always use a *written* list of needs.
— Try to conserve gas by buying food for a longer time period and in larger quantities.
— Avoid buying when hungry (especially if you're a "sugarholic").
— Use a calculator, if possible, to total purchases.
— Reduce or eliminate paper products—paper plates, cups, napkins, etc. (Use cloth napkins.)
— Evaluate where to purchase sundry items such as shampoo, mouthwash, etc.(These are normally somewhat cheaper at chain drug store sales.)
— Avoid processed and sugar-coated cereals. (These are expensive and have little nutritional value.)

PRACTICAL APPLICATIONS

— Avoid prepared foods, such as TV dinners, pot pies, cakes, etc. (You are paying for expensive labor that you can provide.)

— Determine good meat cuts that are available from roasts or shoulders and have the butcher cut these for you. (Buying steaks by the package on sale is fairly inexpensive also.)

— Try house brand canned products. (These are normally cheaper and just as nutritious.)

— Avoid products in a cyclical price hike. Substitute or eliminate.

— Shop for advertised specials. (These are usually posted in the store window.)

— Avoid stores that give merchandise stamps if their prices reflect the cost of the stamps. (Not all do— some simply substitute stamps for other advertising.)

— Purchase milk, bread, eggs, etc. from specialty outlet stores if available, as prices are usually 10-15% lower. (Keep some dry milk on hand to reduce "quick" trips to the store.)

— Avoid buying *non-grocery* items in a grocery supermarket except on sale. (These are normally "high mark-up" items.)

— For baby foods, use normal foods processed through a blender.

— *Leave the children at home* to avoid unnecessary pressure.

— Check *every* item as it is being "rung up" at the store and again when you get home.

— Consider canning fresh vegetables whenever possible. Make bulk purchases with other families at farmers' markets and such. (NOTE: Secure canning supplies during off seasons.)

C. *Automobiles* (13% of net income).

The advertising media refers to us as "consumers" but that's not always the best description. I believe that P. T.

PRACTICAL APPLICATIONS

Barnum had a more apt word—suckers. Often we are unwise in our decision-making when it comes to our machines—especially cars.

Many families will buy new cars they cannot afford and trade them long before their utility is depleted. Those who buy a new car, keep it for less than four years and then trade it for a new model have wasted the maximum amount of money. Some people, such as salesmen that drive a great deal, need new cars frequently; most of us do not. We swap cars because we *want* to—not because we *have* to. Many factors enter here such as ego, esteem, maturity, etc. But few Christians seek God's will for the purchase of cars and so they suffer later because of the financial strains placed on home finances.

Budget hints for automobiles:

Buying automobiles.
  — Evaluate your reason for trading. Are you simply "tired" of your present car? (When you get that "car bug," the old machine will appear to be falling apart.)
  — Can your present car be repaired without great expense? How many miles are left in it?
  — Do you *really* need a brand new car, or will a used one do? (Unless the purchase is for business use, the new car may be unnecessary.)
  — What does your budget say about a new car?
  — Do you still owe on your present car? (If you do and you finance the new car, you are paying the maximum interest rate again.)
  — Pay cash if possible. Otherwise, secure your own loan outside the car dealership and bargain as if on a cash basis. Consider buying on a "no trade-in" basis and selling your old car privately.)
  — If it is a used car, talk to the previous owner *before* you buy. (Most people will tell you honestly about

183

PRACTICAL APPLICATIONS

their car if you ask.)
- Bargain for a short term 100% guarantee on a used car. (Avoid any percentage contract—you will lose.)
- Do not be pressured by sale tactics. Set your own price and type of car desired and be willing to lose the "good deals" which require quick decisions.
- Be willing to accept minor difficulties on a used car to secure substantial price reductions. (Be sure you anticipate these repairs.)
- If buying a new car, avoid purchasing a new model when they first come out. (Buy year-end close-outs or demonstrators.)
- A cheaper model with the same options as the luxury model will provide *substantial* savings (just a little less prestige).
- Avoid the use of credit life insurance. It is expensive and unnecessary if you have an adequate insurance program.
- Avoid new car leases except where extremely high mileage is required and a substantial tax saving is offered as well.

Maintaining cars.

- Learn to perform the routine maintenance: oil change, lubrication, tune-up, etc. (The purchase of approximately $25 worth of tools will return at least $100 per year in service costs and repair bills.)
- Repair minor conditions yourself and do them immediately. Do not let "little" problems pile up or you will be tempted to trade cars.
- Purchase oil, grease, spark plugs, points, etc. from a wholesale distributor. Use best grades only and try to combine purchases with two or more friends for best buys.
- Use a *written* maintenance chart for every car and attend to routine maintenance diligently. *Regular*

184

maintenance will extend the life of a car 30-40%.
- Look into purchasing "take-off" tires from dealers who service fleet cars and cars owned by government agencies. First line radial tires are available that provide more mileage than most second line new tires.
- Check your car's gasoline rating and use the cheapest gasoline recommended.

D.   *Debts* (7% of net income).

It would be great if most budgets included 7% debts or less. Unfortunately, the norm in American families is far in excess of this amount. As previously discussed, credit cards, bank loans and installment credit have made it possible for families to go deeply into debt. What things can you do once this situation exists?

- Destroy *all* of your credit cards as a first step.
- Establish a payment schedule that includes all creditors.
- Contact all creditors, honestly relate your problems and arrange an equitable repayment plan.
- Buy on a cash basis and sacrifice your wants and desires until you are *current.*

E.   *Insurance* (6% of net income).

It is unfortunate to see so many families misled in this area. Few people understand insurance, either how much is needed or what kind is necessary. Almost no one would allow someone to sell him a Rolls Royce when he could afford only a Chevrolet; yet, many purchase high cost insurance when their needs dictate otherwise.

Insurance should be used as supplementary *provision* for the family, not protection or profit. An insurance plan is not designed for saving money or for retirement. Ask anyone who assumed it was; the ultimate result was disillusionment and disappointment.

Do not allow someone else to decide what and how much you need. Select insurance based on God's plan for *your* life. (Figure 2 will help you analyze your needs.)

In our society, insurance *can* be used as an inexpensive vehicle to provide future family income and thus release funds today for family use and the Lord's work. In excess, this same insurance can put a family in debt, steal the Lord's money and transfer dependence to the world.

One of your best insurance assets is to have a trustworthy agent in charge of your program. A good insurance agent is usually one who can select from several different companies to provide you with the best possible buy and who will create a brief, uncomplicated plan to analyze your exact needs.

Christians must learn to be prudent and creative in the area of insurance just as in any other purchase. A prudent application of insurance can help avoid calamitous financial debt by *reasonable* purchases in the following areas:

1.   *Adequate insurance for personal liability in home, auto and business.*   A good rule to follow here is to assume liability protection is for the *injured* party and provide enough to protect *his* interest. Law suits of $100,000-$300,000 are the rule today rather than the exception. Coverage extending to these limits increases premiums only moderately.

    a. *Automobile Coverage* - Secure estimates from at least three major insurance companies before purchasing. As stated in a previous section, evaluate as follows:

        — Select adequate liability coverage.

        — Consider collision and comprehensive coverage.

        (NOTE: One important factor here is: Can you afford to have your car repaired if you have an accident where you are at fault?)

        — The need for medical benefits, etc.

        — Use at least $100 deductibles with above.

    b. *Home Coverage* - Secure at least three estimates as stated above. Normally, this type of insurance can best be satisfied with a comprehensive package (homeowners, renters policy, etc.). Use of the deductible feature will substantially reduce premiums.

c. *Business Coverage* - Secure estimates as stated above. Again, a package plan usually provides the best coverage at the least cost. A reliable insurance agent who understands your business is essential here.

2. *Adequate life insurance.* Considering the low cost of death provision, a Christian should evaluate life insurance, especially where there are minor children involved. Proper provision for the family involves carrying sufficient insurance to remove the burden from others if possible. This *does not* mean that God dies with you and, therefore, every contingency must be covered.

The discussion often arises about term insurance versus permanent or "whole life" insurance. Generally, unless insurance premiums can be tax deductible, term insurance is far less costly. The principle to observe is to purchase insurance for *provision,* not *investment.* Insurance cash reserves typically yield 3-4% interest (a poor return at best). Therefore, purchase what is required at the least cost.

Term insurance is now available which extends to 65 or 70 years of age and will probably be extended further, but as age advances, the need for insurance normally diminishes. If whole life policies are in existence, a thorough analysis should be made by a qualified insurance agent to determine whether the policies should remain in force or be converted. Particular attention should be given to at least borrowing the cash reserve of the policy and reinvesting in a secure, higher interest program.

PRACTICAL APPLICATIONS

3.   *Major medical insurance.*   Except for the chronically ill with pre-existing coverage, hospitalization insurance is generally a poor expenditure. (The exception to this would be "group" insurance policies. These normally provide inexpensive, broad range medical coverage.) However, major medical insurance that will pay most costs involved in serious illnesses is relatively inexpensive. For example, insurance paying 80% of medical expenses, for a family of five, costs under $300 per year.

F.   *Recreation-entertainment* (6% of net income).

We are a recreation-oriented country. That is not necessarily bad if put in the proper perspective. But those who are in debt cannot use their creditor's money to entertain themselves. The normal tendency is to escape problems, even if only for a short while—even if the problems then become more acute. Christians must resist this urge and control recreation and entertainment expenses while in debt.

What a terrible witness it is for a Christian who is already in financial bondage to indulge himself at the expense of others. God knows we need rest and relaxation, and He will often provide it from unexpected sources once our *attitude* is correct. Every believer, whether in debt or not, should seek to reduce entertainment expenses. This can usually be done without sacrificing family quality time.

Recreation hints:

— Plan vacations during "off seasons" if possible.
— Consider a camping vacation to avoid motel and food expenses. (Christian friends can pool the expense of camping items.)
— Select vacation areas in your general locale.
— Consider swapping residences with a Christian family

   — in another locale to provide an inexpensive vacation.
   — Use some family games in place of movies. (Like some of those unused games received at Christmas.)
   — Consider two or more families taking vacation trips together to reduce expense and increase fellowship.
   — If flying, use the least expensive coach fare (i.e., late night or early morning usually saves 10-20%).

G.   *Clothing* (5% of net income).

Many families in debt sacrifice this area in their budget because of excesses in other areas. And yet, with prudent planning and buying, your family can be clothed neatly without great expense. This requires *effort* on your part in terms of:

1. Saving enough money to buy without using credit.
2. Educating family members on care of clothing.
3. Applying discipline with children to enforce these habits.
4. Developing skills in making and mending clothing.

Learn to be utilizers of our resources rather than consumers. How many families have closets full of clothes they no longer wear because they are "out of style"?

Many families with large surplus incomes spend excessively in the area of clothes. Assess whether it really matters that you have all of the latest styles. Do your purchases reflect good utility rather than ego? Do you buy clothes to satisfy a need or a desire?

Budget Hints:

   — Make as many of the children's clothes as time will allow. (Average savings is 50-60%.)
   — Make a *written* list of clothing needs and purchase during the "off" season as much as possible.
   — Select outfits that can be mixed and used in multiple combinations rather than as a single set.
   — Frequent the discount outlets which carry unmarked

"name brand" goods.
- Frequent authentic factory outlet stores for close-out values of top quality.
- Select home washable fabrics in new clothes.
- Use coin-operated dry cleaning machines instead of commercial cleaners.
- Practice early repair for damaged clothing. Learn to utilize all clothing fully (especially children's wear).

H.   *Medical-dental expenses (5% of net income).*

You must anticipate these expenses in your budget and set aside funds regularly; failure to do so will wreck your plans and lead to indebtedness. Do not sacrifice family health due to lack of planning, but at the same time, do not use doctors excessively. Proper prevention is much cheaper than correction. You can avoid many dental bills by teaching children to eat the right foods and clean their teeth properly. Your dentist will supply all the information you need on this subject. Many doctor bills can be avoided in the same way. Take proper care of your body through diet, rest and exercise, and it will respond with good health. Abuse your body and you must ultimately pay through illnesses and malfunctions. This is not to say that all illnesses or problems are caused by neglect, but a great many are.

Do not be hesitant to question doctors and dentists in advance about costs. Also, educate yourself enough to discern when you are getting good value for your money. Most ethical professional men will not take offense at your questions. If they do, that may be a hint to change services.

In the case of prescriptions, shop around. You will be amazed to discover the wide variance in prices from one store to the next. Ask about cash discounts, too. Many stores will give 5-10% off for cash purchases.

PRACTICAL APPLICATIONS

I.   *Savings* (5% of net income).

It is important that some savings be established in the budget. Otherwise, the use of credit becomes a lifelong necessity and debt a way of life. Your savings will allow you to purchase items for cash and shop for the best buys, irrespective of the store.

Savings hints:

— Use a company payroll withdrawal, if possible. This removes the money before you receive it.
— Use an automatic bank withdrawal from you checking account.
— Write your savings account a check just as if it were a creditor.
— When an existing debt is paid off, reallocate that money to savings.

J.   *Variable household expenses.*

These can include a myriad of items. Some of the expenses occur monthly while others occur on an as-needed basis (such as appliances).

One of the most important factors in home expenses is *you.* If you can perform routine maintenance and repair, considerable expenses can be avoided. Many people rationalize not doing these things on the basis that their time is too valuable; that is nonsense. If every hour of the day is tied up in the pursuit of money then, as previously defined, you're in bondage. A part of care and maintenance around the home relates to family life, particularly the training of children. When they see mom and dad willing to do some physical labor to help around the home, they will learn good habits. But if you refuse to get involved, why should they? Where will they ever learn the skills of self-sufficiency?

Some men avoid working on home projects because they say they lack the necessary skills. Well, those skills are *learned,* not *gifted.* There are many good books that detail every area of home maintenance. As previously mentioned, at some point in the future many of these skills will be necessities rather than choices.

Budget hints:

1. *Reducing household appliances costs.*
   a. *Maintaining existing units.*
   — Review service manuals for ordinary maintenance care and perform as often as required.
   — Keep a *written* maintenance chart on or near the unit.
   — Purchase a shop manual from manufacturer. (Most major manufacturers will sell this upon written request.)
   — Utilize the unit within suggested standards. (Example: Do not overload washers and dryers.)
   — If a unit out-of-warranty breaks down, use the fix-it guide to determine problem and repair if possible. *Before* calling outside service, seek free counsel from Christian friends (often someone you know is a fix-it type).
   — Before discarding the old unit for a new one, consider an overhaul of the existing machine.
   b. *Purchasing appliances.*
   — Utilize a consumer buying guide to determine the best manufacturer.
   — Select a unit based on functional use and not on dials and gadgets. (Deluxe models cost more but do not perform better and usually require more maintenance.)
   — Shop around and compare prices on the leading products. (Keep a written record of findings.)
   — Look for volume dealers who carry name brand products under their own label.
   — Purchase the item on a cash basis without a trade-

in (the seller will discount for cash without trade).
- Avoid dealer service contracts. They are some-times expensive and often frustrating. (If the product warranty is not sufficient, look for another brand.)
- Insist on *free* delivery and installation. (Dealer may resist, but will probably agree.)
- Look for similar used units in the paper or shopper's guide.

2. *Reducing furniture costs.*
- Consult a consumer buying index for best pur-chase value.
- Consider repairing and rebuilding used furniture of good quality. (Many good fix-it guides explain how to refinish and reupholster furniture.)
- Consult local shopper's guide for good quality buys.
- Shop local "garage" sales.
- Shop for discontinued furniture lines.

3. *Reducing "fixed" budget items.*
   a. *Saving on the telephone bill.*
- Evaluate the need for more than one telephone (how many calls received at night, convenience versus cost, etc.). Use a standard telephone in place of a special model.
- Use a three-minute egg timer for long distance calls. (Be willing to schedule only three-minute calls to your family.)
- Call long distance during reduced hours when-ever possible.
- Limit the number of calls by strict agreement.
- Keep a *written* long distance phone log (date, time, duration) next to each telephone.
- Write letters instead of calling frequently. (Letters show more real consideration sometimes anyway.)

PRACTICAL APPLICATIONS

b. *Keeping the cost of electricity down.*
- With air conditioning or heating, check attic insulation, windows for air leaks, system filters (clean regularly), doors for air leaks, excessive glass exposure, etc.
- Attic insulation of at least 6" depth will save 10% in heating and air conditioning costs.
- Keep thermostats set at moderate comfort (68-70 degrees in winter; 74-78 degrees in summer).
- Delay using heating or air conditioning units until obvious discomfort is noticed.
- Lower system use when the house is vacant for eight hours or more.
- Use blankets instead of furnace for nighttime comfort.
- Close all vents in unused rooms and most of upstairs vents in two-story dwellings.
- Turn off unused lights; reduce bulb wattage in areas used only for "effect" lighting.
- Purchase 130 volt light bulbs. (They will last five times longer—normally available at electric company outlet stores.)
- Coordinate baths to conserve hot water. (Approximately 10% of hot water in the tank is used to heat the lines to bathrooms. Heat these lines as seldom as possible.)
- Insulate all exposed hot water lines.
- Optimize use of dishwasher, clothes washer and dryer. (Fill them to capacity—but not over.)
- Stop dishwasher before drying cycle periodically. (Dishes dry normally from heat of previous wash cycle.)
- Use the cooking oven only for large food items. Coordinate baking to utilize the heated oven.
- Unplug "instant on" TV's at night and if away for six hours or more (instant on means constantly on).

c. Reducing home care costs.

— Purchase a home sprayer for lawn spraying and pest control. It costs $25 but will save $200-$300 over a three-year period.

— Reduce substantially your use of fertilizers and hybrid seed. Practice organic cultivation of grass and shrubs (i.e., use natural fertilizer from dairies, chicken farms, etc.).

— Utilize rental steam cleaner for carpets. For the average home that will cost $20 as opposed to $75-$100 for professional carpet service.

— Use water base flat enamel paint in high traffic areas. (It is washable and durable and easy to apply. Always use a high quality product.)

4. *Lowering costs in general areas of budgeting.*

— Shop for bank services where checking accounts are without cost. Even if you must bank by mail, the slight inconvenience will save $60-100 per year.

— All pets cost money. Limit your pets to those you *really* care for and the family enjoys.

— Try reducing periodical subscriptions (newspapers, magazines, books, records, etc.). Before subscribing, purchase them at a store to evaluate how useful they are to you. Once you determine to subscribe to a periodical, longer contracts (2-3 years) provide a substantial saving.

5. *Deciding whether to borrow in order to buy.*

— Avoid borrowing for highly depreciable or consumable items (pleasure cars, appliances, furniture, vacations, food, etc.). If you purchase these items for "cash" you will always be in a better bargaining position.

— Borrowing for household items such as appliances can bind you financially. You may find it difficult to escape the borrowing trap because of payments on the existing loans.

— Interest on credit card loans may exceed 50%* per year. (Due to interest compounded on delinquent payments.)

— Installment loans may exceed 12%* per year and carry substantial prepayment penalties.

— Collateralized personal loans are generally the least costly method of financing.

— Credit life insurance on loans may cost two-three times as much as the equivalent amount in term life insurance.

Summary

At this point, you have the necessary tools to establish your own budget. Only one additional ingredient is necessary—desire. No budget will implement itself; it requires effort on your part and good *communication* in the family.

Living on a budget is not only prudent, but it can be fun. As you have successes in various areas, share them with others. Challenge your children as well. Establish budget goals for them and rewards for achievement.

The following is a summarized list of the financial principles applicable to home financial planning. Study these and apply them. Then share God's blessings with others around you.

1. *Principles dealing with home finances.*
   A. Use a written plan.
   B. Provide for the Lord's work first.
   C. Excel at your tasks.
   D. Limit credit!

* Usually determined by state law.

E. Think before buying:
  - Is it necessary?
  - Does it reflect your Christian ethic?
  - Is it the best buy?
  - Is it an impulse item?
  - Does it add to or detract from the family?
  - Is it a highly depreciable item?
  - Does it require costly upkeep?
F. Practice saving money regularly.
G. Set your own goals—with your family.
H. Get out of debt!
I. Limit business involvement.
J. Avoid indulgences, lavishness.
K. Seek good Christian counsel.
L. Stick to your plans!

2. *Purpose of a budget.*
  A. To define income vs. expense.
  B. To detect problem areas.
  C. To provide a written plan.
  D. To aid in follow-up.
  E. To schedule money in and out of the home.

3. *What a budget will do.*
  A. Help you visualize your goals.
  B. Provide a written point of reference for husband and wife.
  C. Help family communications.
  D. Provide a written reminder.
  E. Tattle on your habits.

4. *What a budget will not do.*
  A. Solve your immediate problems.
  B. Make you *use* it.
  C. Take the place of action!

5. *How to:*

PRACTICAL APPLICATIONS

A. Calculate actual expenses.
   - Use a 30-day expense diary (notebook).
   - Use a checking account ledger.
   - Use a creditor ledger showing each debt due.
B. Make out a family budget.
   - Define actual expenditures (present budget).
   - Define proposed expenditures (future budget).
   - Calculate income.
   - Calculate fixed expenses.
   - Calculate variable expenses.
C. Use a budget.
   - Post it out in the open!
   - Set an achievable goal.
   - Keep it up-to-date.
   - Establish a set time and day to review it.

NOTE: A workbook series on Christian finances is also available for those who would like to study and/or teach these principles. Please contact your local Christian bookstore and ask for *Christian Financial Concepts — God's Principles of Handling Money*.

PRACTICAL APPLICATIONS

Figure 1 — Family Budgeting

Income Per Month		Payments Per Month	
Salary	_____	1. Tithe	$_____
Rents	_____	2. Taxes	_____
Notes	_____	3. Housing	
Interest	_____	(a) Payments	_____
Dividends	_____	(b) Lawn	_____
Other	_____	(c) Maintenance	_____
Income tax		(d) Pool, etc.	_____
returned	_____	(e) Taxes	_____
		4. Food	
Total		(a) Groceries	_____
(less) tax*	_____	(b) Milk, bread	_____
		(c) Sundry items	_____
		5. Auto	
Net income	_____	(a) Payments	_____
		(b) Gasoline	_____
Net monthly		(c) Maintenance	
income	$_____	8¢ per mile	_____
		6. Utilities	
		(a) Electricity	_____
		(b) Gas	_____
		(c) Water	_____
		(d) Garbage	_____
		(e) Telephone	_____
		(f) Other	_____
		7. Insurance	
		(a) Auto	_____
		(b) Health	_____
		(c) Life	_____
		(d) Other	_____
		8. Loans	
* Not applicable if net		(a) Major	_____
income is used.		(b) Credit card	_____
		(c) Installments	_____

PRACTICAL APPLICATIONS

Figure 1 — Family Budgeting - continued

<u>INCOME VS. EXPENSE</u>

Net monthy
   income $_____

Less
   expenses $_____

Overage: $_____

    (d) Other   _____
9. Entertainment-
   recreation   _____
10. Clothing   _____
11. Savings   _____
12. Medical   _____
   (a) Dentist   _____
   (b) Doctor   _____
   (c) Other   _____
13. Miscellaneous   _____

                 _____

PRACTICAL APPLICATIONS

Figure 2 — Insurance Needs

1. Present income per year $ _____

2. Life insurance   (_____) premiums per yr.

3. Savings per year (_____)

4. Investments   (_____) per year

5. Est. living costs for husband per year   (_____)

6. Other deductions per year   (_____)

7. Total   (_____)

8. Income required per year (subtract step 7 from step 1) $ _____

9. Company retirement, social security, etc. supplied upon husband's death   _____

10. Investment income, other   _____

11. Wife's, children's income   _____

PRACTICAL APPLICATIONS

Figure 2 — Insurance Needs - continued

12.   Total   (_____)
     (Steps 8-11)

13. Income pro- $_____
    vision needed
    per year (Subtract
    step 12 from step 7)

NOTE 1 — Multiply line 13 by 18=approximate insurance necessary to continue present standard of living with no asset reduction.

NOTE 2 — Add to this amount allowance for college or business.

NOTE 3 — Total amount needed will vary if provision is anticipated for a *fixed* number of years only.

Example: $100,000 insurance needed to generate a $10,000 per year income. Income earning rate est. = 6%.
At the end of a 10-year period, approximately $43,000 of insurance remains.